HOUSING FINANCE

a basic guide

Henry Aughton
and
Peter Malpass

Fourth revised edition

Shelter
THE NATIONAL CAMPAIGN FOR HOMELESS PEOPLE

Fourth revised edition (First edition published in 1981)
Published in 1994 by Shelter, 88 Old Street, London EC1V 9HU
Registered Co. 1038133. Registered Charity 263710

British Library Cataloguing-in-Publication Data – a catalogue record for this book is available
from the British Library.
ISBN 1 870767 28 4

Cartoons by Brick
Designed by Rahila Gupta, Shelter
Layout by Sue MacDonald, Shelter
Printed by Stanley Hunt, Northamptonshire NN10 9UA

Trade Distribution by Turnaround, 27 Horsell Road, London N5 1XL. Tel: 0171 609 7568

Acknowledgements

Henry Aughton wrote the first two editions of *Housing Finance* and did most of the work on the third edition. It is impossible to overstate the importance of Henry's contribution, beginning with the first edition in 1981 at a time when there was nothing else available for readers who wanted a simple and straightforward explanation of housing finance in Britain. My role in this has been to try to carry forward the spirit of Henry's approach and to produce a new edition which takes account of the many changes in housing finance since 1990.

In producing this new edition I have been supported by Rahila Gupta, Sue MacDonald and Fran Ellery at Shelter. Without their help in turning the old text into a disk the rewriting would have been far more onerous. They have also taken on the task of editing and producing the final version. I am also grateful to Carol Grant, Shelter's Director of Communications, for encouraging me to undertake the work and for overseeing the whole project.

Thanks are due to Henry Aughton for reading through the full text at a late stage, to Kate Duggan for her help on Chapter 5 and to a housing association finance director (who preferred to remain anonymous) for his guidance on aspects of Chapter 3. Richard Lloyd at Shelter kindly provided information on the costs of homelessness. I must add, of course, that none of these people bears any responsibility for any errors that remain in the text.

Peter Malpass
Bristol
June 1994

Note about the authors

Henry Aughton has a background in both housing and finance. He was Hemel Hempstead's Borough Treasurer for 14 years and subsequently Dacorum District Council's first Chief Executive. Altogether, he has had 47 years experience in local government. He was housing adviser to the Association of Municipal Corporations and specialist adviser in 1977 and 1978 to the House of Commons Environment Sub-Committee. He has also served on housing working parties of the Chartered Institute of Public Finance and Accountancy and was, for many years, Deputy Chair of Shelter and Chair of its finance committee. He is currently Honorary Treasurer of the National Housing and Town Planning Council.

Peter Malpass is Professor of Housing Policy at the University of the West of England, Bristol, where he manages the MA in Housing Studies. He has been involved in housing since 1970, initially as a door to door council rent collector but mainly as a researcher and teacher. He has published widely on many aspects of housing policy and is the co-author of Housing Policy and Practice (now in its fourth edition). He is currently carrying out research for the Housing Corporation on land supply for housing associations, and his other research interests are affordability and the governance of housing associations.

Contents

Chapter 3 – Housing Associations 50

Chapter 4 – The Private Rented Sector 63

Chapter 5 – Housing Benefit 73

Chapter 6 – Owner-occupation 83

Chapter 7 – Reform: A Range of Views 95

Chapter 8 – What Next? 106

Index 111

List of Tables and Figures

Foreword

This basic guide was first published in 1981, and updated in 1986 and 1990. Henry Aughton wrote the first two editions and was the main author of the 1990 edition. This new edition retains much of Henry's approach and his original text. My objective has been largely confined to updating what has proved to be a very popular and successful book.

Housing finance is a fast moving policy area and fundamental changes introduced by the Housing Act 1988 and the Local Government and Housing Act 1989 have now worked their way into the system. Further changes have been made, affecting subsidy for private renting and the level of support for mortgaged home owners. Reform of tax relief appeared to be out of the question in 1990 but now the Chancellor seems to be set on phasing it out by the end of the century. Thus a new edition of the basic guide was required.

The purpose of this guide, like its earlier versions, is to describe how housing finance works in England and Wales, and what the future will hold. It is important to say that the scope of the guide is limited to England and Wales; much of what follows is applicable to Scotland and Northern Ireland but, in certain significant respects, the situation and legislation in these parts of the United Kingdom is different.

Housing finance is regarded by most people as impossibly complicated and most published work on the subject, although valuable to housing professionals, may reinforce that perception. Yet the ordinary individual already has, unconsciously, a useful store of background knowledge. Provided that jargon and technicalities are avoided, they can make their own assessment of issues, see how present systems work, and form judgements as to the value of proposed changes.

This guide aims to help in that process. Those seeking professional qualifications may find it a useful beginning. It is aimed at councillors, members of housing association management committees, those working in housing or finance departments, housing advice workers, perhaps even MPs – in fact, anyone who wants to know how the main tenures work and why there are still daunting housing problems.

 **Overview**

What is housing finance?

Housing represents the largest single expenditure item in most household budgets, and so the first thing to say is that housing finance includes the way that households pay for their housing. It is about the ways that rents are fixed and mortgages are provided. What people pay for their housing is affected by government policy, mainly by various tax and subsidy arrangements. Second, house building is an important part of the construction industry, and housing finance includes the ways in which housing production is financed and paid for.

Very large amounts of money spent on housing each year are handled by local authorities and housing associations, and the greatest share of this money counts as public expenditure – over £7.4 billion in 1994/95. To understand housing finance, therefore, we have to look at how housing is used by governments to distribute and control public expenditure as a whole.

Expenditure on housing production and consumption has a big influence on the state of the wider economy, and governments cannot afford to ignore what is happening in the housing market. Indeed they sometimes try to use the housing market as a lever to influence the wider economy.

In considering the financial arrangements for housing, it is necessary first to remember its special characteristics.

Housing – special features

There are two particular characteristics that are of great importance for an understanding of housing finance. First, housing is very expensive to produce – because it requires land, considerable amounts of materials and many hours of labour time. The high cost of housing means that people who cannot afford to buy outright need to have access to it in some other way. What most people do is spread the cost of their housing over long periods. Renting and mortgaged house purchase developed as different ways of allowing people to do so. Another response to high cost is subsidy and much of the debate about housing finance revolves around this issue.

The second key feature is that housing is what economists call a durable commodity, unlike for example food and drink, or semi-durable commodities like cars or washing machines. Its lifespan – for practical purposes only land has a longer life – makes it almost unique. The long life of houses means that they retain their value over many years, and the effect of inflation is particularly important because, over a run of years, the value of houses in money terms actually grows. It is for this reason that housing has come to be seen as a good investment. And over the last 25 years the growth in house prices has been spectacular, even allowing for the falls that have been witnessed since 1990.

There are other factors besides inflation which affect house prices. There is the availability or scarcity of mortgage funds from building societies and banks or the sudden variations of mortgage interest rates. And there is the scarcity of affordable and accessible rented property in many areas which increases the pressure on house prices by obliging numbers of people to buy even when, on any rational view, they cannot really afford it.

The steady pressure of demand for housing, whether for renting or buying, should in theory increase supply. In this way the market, operating freely, is supposed to solve the problem. Unfortunately housing demonstrates another unhelpful characteristic – supply is 'inelastic'. It cannot be increased rapidly, simply because of the time taken to build each house. Another factor affecting the inelasticity of housing supply is that, because of the long timescale of production, prudent builders will only increase supply if they are sure that there will still be adequate demand when the houses are ready. Whatever the demand, the size of the housing stock grows slowly. To increase the total supply by two per cent per annum would require the production of 460,000 dwellings, a figure not even approached in Britain for 25 years. In recent times the annual increase has been well under one per cent.

Housing cannot safely be left to market forces. Before the first world war, before the introduction of rent control, market forces operated. Yet the country faced shortages, slums, overcrowding, disrepair, and lack of basic amenities. Seventy five years of effort since 1919 have raised standards enormously for most people but have never fully overcome the problems. In 1994 council house waiting lists are as long as ever; there are high numbers of families accepted by councils as homeless; and in many cities, large numbers of young single people, not eligible under the law for help as homeless persons and affected by reductions in social security provision, are reduced to sleeping rough. In addition, one in every thirteen houses is unfit for human habitation. It is a shocking indictment of government housing policies in the last 15 years.

Ever since the first world war, it has been accepted that decent housing standards are an essential condition of a just and healthy society, and indeed, are as necessary in an advanced industrial society as effective health, education and welfare services. There was, for much of the period since 1945, national consensus about this, though different parties attached different emphasis at times to various aspects of housing policies.

But alas for good intentions, housing is such a significant element in terms of the resources it requires that governments have never been able to resist using housing policies as tools in their attempts at overall management of the nation's economy.

Visible and invisible subsidies

Over the years housing has been subsidised in various ways. There has been much debate about what counts as housing subsidy and how it should be measured. Most economists prefer to define subsidy as the difference between the price actually charged for an item and the price that it would fetch in a free market. But this can be difficult to measure, because where there is no free market (as has been the case in housing for 80 years) no one can confidently say what that price would be. In practice the debate about housing subsidies has tended to concentrate on a 'cash flow' approach. In council housing this means the amount of money that is provided to make up the difference between the rents charged and the amount necessary to cover expenditure on the housing service.

In Britain, the cost of subsidies to council housing has been a constant topic for government ministers. The cost of subsidising home-ownership, on the other hand, was seldom mentioned and it is only within the last 25 years that it has become widely understood that home-owners are subsidised.

The Treasury maintained for many years that tax relief on mortgages was not a subsidy. It suited them to argue that a subsidy is an actual payment, whereas this was tax forgone – how could it be a subsidy not to take someone's own money away from them? This is very reassuring until it is realised that the effect is precisely the same. The payment of a subsidy increases the disposable income of the fortunate recipient; and so does tax relief.

The economists' view

Academic economists point to two features of housing – the investment aspect which is involved in the provision of a dwelling; and the consumption aspect which is the use and benefit of the accommodation.

With private rented housing, (as with council housing), the landlord bears the cost of provision. This investment results in ownership of an asset which will produce an income – the rent paid by the tenant. The landlord has the ownership, the tenant has the use.

In considering what the rent should be, economists tend to favour market rents or something close to market rents. The rental value of a dwelling is what people are prepared to pay for the use of it, irrespective of what it cost the owner to acquire it. Scarcity of rented accommodation will naturally result in higher rents (unless there is interference with market forces by rent control), and in the view of economists, this is as it should be, for higher rents will eventually increase supply. They contend that where a tenant pays a lower rent, the subsidy is the amount of the difference between the market rent and rent actually paid, and it is a subsidy borne by the landlord.

There are, however, landlords who have not been concerned with profit or with the strictures of market theory. They are local authorities and housing associations, and nowadays they provide over four times as many rented dwellings as do private landlords. Their purpose has always been to meet the housing needs of people who cannot afford to buy or pay the sort of rents which a free market would require. Their primary concern has been to provide housing at rents which the average tenant can pay although such rents may not provide sufficient income to cover the cost of borrowing and of management and maintenance. Hence, the need for housing subsidies whether in the form of annual payments towards the upkeep or payments towards the initial cost of provision.

Central government and housing finance

Governments have always needed to know how much they have to raise and this used to be all they did need to know. In modern times, governments have also attempted, with varying success, to manage the economy. In this they have been concerned, among other things, with the share of the total national income (the Gross Domestic Product) which the public sector, national and local, will absorb. A large part of this sector's needs will be met by taxation and other revenues and the rest was referred to as the Public Sector Borrowing Requirement (PSBR).

Each year a White Paper is published, called *The Government's Expenditure Plans*. This gives details of expenditure for each group of services (defence, social services, education, housing and so on) for the past five years and the current year, and what is planned for the next three years. The various tables cover local authority as well as central government activity. The White Paper became so big that the government now produces (and sells) it in a number of separate volumes, and housing is dealt with in the volume entitled the *DoE Annual Report*.

The enormous mass of figures, analyses and supporting statements is

Table 1   Housing Public Expenditure

	1993/4 estimated outturn	1994/5 plans	1995/6 plans	1996/7 plans
Capital	£m	£m	£m	£m
Housing Corporation net capital	1786.1	1475.3	1436.3	1444.9
LA capital	1432.8	1219.4	1251.6	1317.4
Total capital	3218.9	2694.7	2687.9	2762.3
Revenue				
Housing Corporation and Housing Associations	165.4	207.2	213.2	218.2
Local authorities				
HRA subsidy	4125.0	4381.0	4525.1	4378.5
Other	116.5	119.2	129.8	171.5
Total revenue	4406.9	4707.4	4868.1	4768.2
Total housing	7625.8	7402.1	7556.0	7530.5
Housing Corporation				
Capital				
DoE support				
Capital	1843.1	1533.3	1494.3	1502.9
Other	−57.0	−58.0	−58.0	−58.0
Net capital	1786.1	1475.3	1436.3	1444.9
Revenue				
Grants & subsidies	135.2	177.3	182.7	187.9
Running costs	30.1	29.8	30.4	30.2
Total revenue	165.4	207.2	213.2	218.2

Table 1 Housing Public Expenditure (cont.)

	1993/4 estimated outturn	1994/5 plans	1995/6 plans	1996/7 plans
Local authority				
Capital for housing				
Credit approvals specified capital	1011.0	893.0	927.3	1044.8
Grants (for renovation of private housing, area improvement and slum clearance)	407.9	313.7	311.8	259.3
Other	13.9	12.8	12.4	13.3
Total LA capital	1432.8	1219.4	1251.6	1317.4
Housing revenue account subsidy				
Housing element	877.0	832.0	788.5	712.0
Rent rebate element	3248.0	3549.0	3736.6	3666.5
Total HRA subsidy	4125.0	4381.0	4525.1	4378.5

intended to provide the basis on which the government's fiscal policy (how, and how much, is to be raised in taxes) and its borrowing requirement can be determined. It will also give the information needed for economic management.

Table 1 above shows the main items of public expenditure on housing in the mid 1990s. The figures are taken from the *DoE Annual Report 1994*, Figures 75, 80, 84 and 86.

The public expenditure figures reveal the continuing commitment to housing associations as the major providers of new social rented housing. Until 1992/93 local authority capital programmes had always exceeded those of housing associations. Housing association capital expenditure is mostly used to pay for new building to add to the stock, whereas local authority capital is overwhelmingly used for renovation of the existing stock, both public and private.

When comparing the figures for local authorities and housing associations it is important to remember three key points. First, capital expenditure by the Housing Corporation, which acts as the conduit for government money to housing associations (see chapter 3), is only a part of the total capital expenditure of housing associations and the private finance raised by associations is not shown in the tables. In the case of local authorities, however, the whole of their capital programme counts as public expenditure, and therefore does appear in the tables.

Second, local authorities and housing associations are subsidised in different ways; all the capital expenditure by the Housing Corporation represents subsidy (Housing Association Grant) paid as a lump sum at the time of construction. The figures for capital expenditure by local authorities on their own housing, however, refer to permission to borrow the necessary money. There is no subsidy element in these figures. Central government expenditure here (if any) comes in the form of revenue support towards the costs of repaying loans over a long period. This is included in the housing element of the Housing Revenue Account (HRA) subsidy (see chapter 2).

Third, whilst the figures for HRA subsidy include the cost of rent rebates (housing benefit) paid to council tenants, the housing public expenditure tables do not show the cost of housing benefit paid to housing association tenants. In their case the cost of housing benefit is included in the social security accounts (where it properly belongs).

One other glaring omission from the Housing Programme is any mention of the tax relief for owner-occupiers though it is now generally acknowledged that mortgage interest tax relief is a subsidy to house purchase. The cost of this was never actually included in the programme totals but it was at least given reasonable prominence in a note that followed. This has been discontinued and the *DOE Annual Report 1994* makes no reference to the subject of mortgage interest relief. To discover the level of assistance provided through mortgage interest relief it is necessary to look in a separate volume altogether.

Then there is another important tax concession – the exemption from capital gains tax on house sales. The gross cost of this, estimated at £6,000m in 1987-88, leaps to a staggering £10,000m for 1988-89 as house prices spiralled upwards.

This chapter has drawn attention to the need to look at housing finance in relation to public expenditure as a whole. The details of the British housing finance system, however, vary from one tenure to another. Subsequent chapters look at the arrangements in council housing, housing associations, private renting and owner occupation. In looking at individual tenures it is important to remember that although the methods of subsidy and so on are different in each, the separate tenures cannot be viewed in isolation; what goes on in one tenure has implications for what happens elsewhere.

2 Council Housing

For practical purposes, council housing did not exist until the responsibility of acting as the main providers of future rented housing was placed on the local authorities by the Housing and Town Planning Act, 1919. Until then a handful of charitable trusts, forerunners of the housing association movement, had built more houses than all the councils put together.

Councils had no experience in large scale housing provision. Other countries faced similar problems but they turned to housing associations. That choice was not open to Britain, whose housing associations were too few, and too small, to be expected to deal effectively with the colossal tasks which this country faced in the aftermath of the first world war. The decision of the then coalition government, and every successive government until 1979, to place the responsibility for providing and managing rented housing on the local authorities, has been more than justified by their achievements.

Let us consider then, the way that councils operate as housing authorities, and the statutory and financial institutions which govern their actions.

Providing the houses

Houses are built on borrowed money. An individual buys or builds with the help of a loan, usually from a building society or a bank, paid back with interest over a period of probably 25 years. Councils also pay for their houses through loans, but repayment is 60 years – the assumed life of a house.

Governments invariably set down the period within which loans raised by a council must be repaid. Councils can repay over a shorter period if they wish but most go for the longest term available. They are anxious to keep annual loan charges (interest on the loans plus an element of repayment of the principal) down to a minimum.

Repayment was by what is called the sinking fund method, a formula which means a very small repayment of principal in the first year. In each year that follows, the sum to be repaid is worked out by adding five per cent to the previous year's payment. The starting point was calculated so that by the sixtieth year, the whole loan would have been repaid. Interest on the outstanding loan decreases a little each year since it was payable on a declining amount. It was rather like the annuity method used with building society mortgage loans (unless these are of the endowment type); principal repayments gradually increase, interest payments gradually decline.

Capital expenditure

In providing houses, it is necessary to incur expenditure on land, roads, sewers, and of course, the buildings themselves. The expenditure on the acquisition of these permanent assets is called capital expenditure (as distinct from recurring annual expenditure such as running costs and loan charges, which is revenue expenditure). The transactions involved are recorded in a housing capital account, showing on the expenditure side what has been spent on land, roads, sewers, construction and preparation costs, and on the income side the loans raised to finance the operation and any capital receipts (from the sale of houses or land) which have been used to meet some of the expenditure. There may also be contributions from revenue but these are likely to be small.

Where the loans come from

A council has many services besides housing which need loans to finance capital spending. Instead of letting each service raise its own loans, it has a Loans Fund, which raises money from financial institutions, the government's Public Works Loan Board, companies, and individuals. The Loans Fund acts as a lender to whichever department needs to borrow for capital spending. This is a great accounting and administrative convenience and has other important advantages. The Loans Fund borrows most of its money for fixed terms of anything from two to sixty years. Only a small proportion of the Loan Fund requirements will be met by 'temporary' borrowing – money repayable at short notice – so unlike a building society there is no problem of rapid withdrawals of large amounts when interest rate changes make other forms of investment more attractive. The bulk of the money will have been borrowed for long periods at fixed rates of interest and the average rate of interest on the total borrowings of any local authority will change only slightly each year. The method provides great stability.

The Loans Fund has to pay interest, of course, to all those from whom it has borrowed. It recharges this interest, at an average rate (called the loans pool rate) to all the services which owe it money. Each year, it gets back from each of the services, like housing, the interest on the loans and an appropriate amount of repayment of principal.

Government control of capital spending

It seems rather difficult to believe these days that until 1976 there was no direct restriction on the number of houses any council chose to build and no council ever used this freedom irresponsibly. Consent to borrow on each scheme, called a loan sanction, had to be sought but as long as this complied with government guidelines on building costs, a loan sanction would not be refused. However, in 1976 there was a financial crisis, which provoked the need to seek an International Monetary Fund loan on terms which required a reduction in public expenditure. From then on, the government took control over the amount of housing that councils could provide, at first, by the loan sanction process.

Loan sanctions disappeared in 1978. Instead, each council had to produce a Local Housing Strategy (LHS) setting out the need in its area for new council building and other housing projects. On the basis of this, it then had to draw up a Housing Investment Programme (HIP), showing what it planned to spend on the items covered by the strategy. The DoE then considered both and allocated borrowing permission for a total sum, instead of for individual items.

At first, the new HIP system was well received – it was a simpler method of cost control and the common sense of local strategy planning was obvious. But while councils were saved a lot of work, central government had acquired new and sweeping powers to control capital spending on housing which it began to use in an arbitrary and blundering fashion. HIP allocations were suddenly cut in June 1979, three months into the financial year. And in February 1980, a moratorium on spending was suddenly announced.

In the meantime, the Local Government, Planning and Land Act, 1980 created a further restriction by shifting control from borrowing to expenditure. Instead of a block allocation of borrowing permission, there was, from

1981-82 onwards, a block allocation of permitted capital expenditure.

There was another confusion. The sale of council houses from 1980 on-wards was beginning to produce large capital receipts. Half of these were intended to be available as an addition to the HIP allocation. But until sales took place, councils had no idea how much extra this would allow them to spend. Investment fell even further as they underestimated what they could spend. By the autumn of 1982 councils were being urged to spend more on council housing. It was, to say the least, a remarkable exercise in financial management.

This display of a profligacy was short-lived. From April 1984, the proportion of capital receipts which could be used was reduced to 40 per cent and reduced again to 20 per cent in 1985. Central government control over the housing programme had increased enormously.

Revenue expenditure

When a scheme is built, capital expenditure ceases. From then on, there will be continued spending on management, repairs, loan charges and other items. This recurring expenditure is known as revenue expenditure and is met from the rents charged, housing subsidies (if any), interest on capital receipts and mortgage interest from the sale of council houses. (These two last items are described in more detail later). Until 1990, there could also be a contribution from councils' own tax income (the rates). This was compulsory if the housing revenue account would otherwise have been in deficit.

All these transactions were shown in a housing revenue account (HRA) which every housing authority had to keep in a form prescribed by the Department of the Environment. The prescribed form of the HRA was significantly changed as a result of the Local Government and Housing Act, 1989, a fact which needs to be borne in mind when making comparisons with years before 1990/91. Table 2 (below) shows a typical HRA in the current format.

Table 2   Typical Housing Revenue Account*

Expenditure		£000
Net debit for loan charges, 'item 8 debit'		2,780
Revenue contributions to capital outlay		–
Supervision & management		
– general	855	
– special	<u>496</u>	1,351
Repairs & maintenance		2,956
HRA rent rebates		4,240
Provision for irrecoverable rent arrears		15
Transfer to general fund		–
Rents, rates, taxes payable on HRA property		112
Other		–
		11,454
Working balance at end of year		607
Total		12,061
Income		
Gross rents		
– dwellings		8,565
– other property		338
Net HRA subsidy		1,816
Net credit from interest & loan charges (item 8 credit)		215
Transfer from general fund		—
Other income		117
		11,051
Working balance at start of year		1,010
Total		12,061

* HRA estimates for 1994/95 for a non-metropolitan authority with 6,000 dwellings.

Rents

The rents of council houses have always been set by local authorities themselves, albeit with some guidance from central government. Differences in rents from one authority to another were mainly due to differing land and building costs at the time when houses were built; local political influence was not generally a key factor. In the past critics tended to highlight differences in rents in apparently similar authorities next door to each other but the Conservative government in the late 1980s focused on what was seen as the insufficient variation in council rents from one region to another, especially when compared with the way that house prices varied across the country. Government policy since 1990 has been to widen differences in rents and to try to make these differences reflect the pattern of house price variation. Thus the average council rent in England in 1993/94 was £32.87 (according to a national survey by the ADC and AMA) but there was also significant regional variation:

— South Yorkshire   £24.38 per week
— Eastern Region   £35.08 per week
— Greater London   £46.63 per week

Regional variations have increased substantially since the introduction of the 1989 Act financial regime in April 1990. This is explained in more detail later in this chapter.

Rent pooling and rent fixing

Similarity in the rents of similar dwellings within a local authority area was achieved by rent pooling. The rents of each separate scheme used to be calculated as each was completed, taking into account annual costs on that scheme (loan charges, repairs and management), and any help with housing subsidy or rate fund contributions. So with different schemes of identical houses there were often significant differences in the rents charged. Many years ago a few of the more progressive councils began to see that the simple solution was to do for the whole stock what they had been doing for each individual scheme – look at the outgoings in total, deduct total subsidies and rate fund contributions, and see what needed to be met by rent income.

Having settled what total income was needed, the council then had to decide what the rents of individual properties should be so that the rent of any dwelling would be seen as fair when compared to others. Every dwelling was assessed for rating purposes for its gross value which was supposed to represent the annual rent that a landlord would expect to receive. Gross values provide a ready made basis of comparing one property with another, reflecting size, quality and location. Most councils used this system or a refined formula of their own.

Where gross rating value was the chosen basis, all the council had to do was calculate the gap between expenditure (on debt charges, management and maintenance) and income from subsidy and rate fund contribution (if any). If that gap was, say, £15 million and the total gross value of all the houses was, say, £10 million then individual rents of one and a half times gross value would produce the required rent income of £15 million to keep the housing account in balance.

The acceptance of rent pooling spread, and became virtually universal in the years following the second world war, as the logic and convenience of the system was recognised. Central government realised that rent pooling transferred the benefit of subsidies on earlier built houses to the later ones which had cost so much more. It would dearly have liked to withdraw subsidies on earlier schemes but settled for taking the effect of rent pooling into account when future subsidy levels were introduced.

Councils listened to the exhortations of government to introduce rebates to help tenants who found even pooled rents a burden and the number of locally operated schemes grew steadily but their effect was usually limited. Most councils felt that income support was a matter for government, not for them; their business was to provide houses at reasonable rents with the help of subsidies.

The rent pooling system, of course, only applies within the area of each local authority. Neighbouring councils have differing average rent levels for reasons of historic accident, such as the proportion of earlier-built low cost houses or the size of the current building programme. The issue produced a lot of discussion in the 1970s and there were advocates of national rent pooling but enthusiasm was lacking amongst councils which might lose slightly, and no government has shown any particular interest.

Subsidies to council housing

There have been two kinds of payment by the Exchequer which affect the housing revenue account. One has been housing subsidy under the Housing Acts, which meets part of housing costs with the object of reducing the amount of rent income which will be required and thus keeping rents down. The other was rent rebate subsidy. This reimbursed a council for rent income lost when it performed a social security function as an agent of the government by giving rent rebates on a means-tested basis to low income tenants. This was relief of poverty, not a housing subsidy.

Perhaps because rent rebates became mandatory under the Housing Finance Act 1972, they (and rent allowances to private tenants) were included in the housing programme of each year's Public Expenditure White Paper until 1982-83 as if they were housing expenditure. In that year they were transferred to the social security programme, where they really belonged. However, in 1990 the costs of housing benefit for council tenants were transferred back into the housing programme as a result of the introduction of a single HRA subsidy (see below).

Subsidies until 1980

The Housing Act 1919 required councils to charge rents which were similar to those of comparable private rented property in the area. The scarcity of comparable new housing in the private sector in the 1920s made council housing an attractive option. Government subsidy bridged the gap between outgoings and rent income with a very modest contribution from the rates. The scheme was generous and produced a lot of houses of excellent quality. But the Treasury disliked it intensely because of the open-ended nature of the subsidy and within three years the scheme was scrapped. No more was heard of deficiency-type subsidies for over 50 years.

Every few years another Housing Act was passed, giving a new scale of subsidies based on annual lump sums per dwelling for future building, and leaving earlier subsidies unchanged. Councils had to make rate fund contributions to qualify for subsidy. This was discontinued in 1956 but most councils went on giving some help from the rates to keep rent levels within the reach of their tenants.

The next change was in 1967 when a new Act gave an annual sum per dwelling on future building which recognised the effect of differences in building costs and higher interest rates – a great improvement.

Everything changed with the Conservative government's Housing Finance Act 1972. For over 50 years councils had enjoyed considerable freedom in rent fixing. Subsidies had been fixed cash sums per dwelling per year and total rent income was the amount necessary to balance the HRA. There then emerged the view that rents should be fixed according to the current value of each property, with subsidy being based on the gap (if any) between aggregate rent income and total expenditure. This was the principle which underlay the 1972 Act and local councils were instructed to determine 'fair rents' for all their houses. The idea was that rents in all tenures, including private and housing association dwellings, would be set on the basis of moderated market rents.

Existing subsidies would be withdrawn quickly and replaced by a deficit subsidy. The thinking was that rising rents would usually cover both rising costs and the effect of withdrawal of the old subsidies. Where they did not, the new subsidy would meet a large part of any shortfall. And since it was believed that steep rent increases would soon produce surpluses, the government proposed to take a share of the surplus.

It was recognised that many tenants would not be able to pay the much higher rents without help, so a rent rebate system, an advance on the pioneering work of some local authorities, was made compulsory for all councils.

All this was reform with a vengeance and it aroused sharper controversy than at any time since councils first became involved with housing. One council, Clay Cross in Derbyshire, refused to implement the Act, and councillors were removed from office, surcharged for the rent income lost and a commissioner was appointed to run the housing service.

The incoming Labour government in 1974 immediately froze rents for a year, and then repealed the fair rent provision for council housing; it restored freedom in rent fixing to local councils, continued what old subsidies remained, and replaced the deficit subsidy with a new temporary subsidy related to the cost of new borrowing. A comprehensive review of housing finance was set up, leading eventually to the consultation document, *Housing Policy* (Cmnd. 6851) in 1977.

The whole purpose of the review was to deal with housing finance in all tenures instead of treating council housing in isolation. In the event the private rented sector was to be reviewed by another committee; the owner-occupied sector was not seen as needing any changes; housing associations were not mentioned except for a comment that council house subsidies should apply to them too; and once again, proposals for the reform of council housing finance were made in isolation.

The main proposals to emerge from the review were that for each local authority area there should be a local housing strategy (LHS), and a housing investment programme (HIP) (described earlier), a tenants' charter, and a new subsidy system.

The proposed new subsidy system was another version of a deficit subsidy. Existing subsidies would continue. Housing costs, it was assumed, would go on rising but rents could reasonably go on rising too, in line with rising earnings. And where rising costs were not covered by rising rents and a reasonable increase in rate fund contributions, the new subsidy would meet the shortfall. But before the new system could be put into effect – apart from the LHS and HIP schemes which had been introduced at once – the Labour government was replaced by the 1979 Conservative government.

The Housing Act 1980

The new government took on Labour's proposed new subsidy system with great enthusiasm although, of course, they modified it to reflect their own ideological preferences; the key change was to empower the Secretary of State to force council rents to rise much faster than wages or prices. The Housing Act, 1980 included existing subsidies, rents and rate fund contributions as the starting point of the new system. The key to it was that the *actual* subsidy that an authority was entitled to was based on *notional* changes in HRA income and expenditure. On the one hand, this approach gave central government control of total Exchequer subsidy expenditure and enabled it to put powerful pressure on rents (via withdrawal of subsidy) whilst, on the other hand, local councils retained some semblance of freedom to set actual rents.

Each year the DoE issued 'determinations' setting out the assumed increases in rents and management and maintenance expenditure. The government assumed that average rents would rise by the prescribed amount though councils could choose to make smaller increases and make up the difference by larger rate fund contributions, or the reverse. It was claimed that the system was a straightforward deficit subsidy which would take care of those justifiable cost increases which would not be covered by reasonable rent or rate fund contribution increases. But, it was also the perfect formula for reducing housing subsidies and for discontinuing them altogether before very long, for the great majority of authorities outside the London area.

In three years, rents more than doubled. But when enormous rent increases resulted in a council being no longer eligible for subsidy, it was not easy to compel it to make further increases for which it saw no justification.

In spite of the pressure on it to increase rents during the 1980s, the public rented sector did better than other tenures, with increases over the period 1982/83 to 1988/89 totalling 39.2 per cent, against 56.1 per cent for housing associations, and 69.8 per cent for private landlords. Housing subsidies to councils, £1,423 million in 1980/81, had been cut to £280 million by 1983/84, but began to increase again and were an estimated £520 million by 1988/89. Still, that was £903 million saved. But alas, the cost of rent rebates rose so steeply – £1,980 million in 1983/84, a planned £2,976 million for 1989/90 – that taking housing and rent rebate subsidies together, the cost to the Exchequer was higher than ever, in spite of all the rent increases.

The sale of council houses

As well as the new subsidy system and rent regime, the 1980 Act contained the right to buy scheme, to fulfil the Conservative party's election pledge to give council tenants the right to buy their houses at a discount.

The right applied to any tenant of three years or more, except for those in dwellings designed or specially adapted for old people. The minimum period has now been reduced to two years. At this point, a tenant of a house has the right to purchase at market value less a discount of 32 per cent, with a further one per cent for every extra year's tenancy up to a maximum of 60 per cent. The discount on flats starts at 40 per cent, and increases at the rate of two per cent at year, reaching a maximum of 70 per cent after 15 years.

Older houses would qualify for full discount, subject to adequate length of tenancy, but the selling price could not be less than the cost to the council of providing the house (the so called 'cost floor'). So, on recently built dwellings which cost a great deal, there could be little or no discount. In any case, there is a £50,000 maximum discount nationally on both houses and flats.

A tenant who could not afford to buy at the time could put down a £100 option to buy within two years at the price fixed at the start. The £100 would be taken off the price or refunded if the tenant still could not afford to buy at the end of two years. As well as the right to buy there was also the right to a council mortgage loan, unless the tenant wanted to get a loan elsewhere.

Councils had previously provided a very useful house purchase finance service which supplemented the facilities given by other lenders and they had always had freedom to fix the terms so long as they did not involve the ratepayers in a loss. They usually charged interest at a quarter or a half per cent above their average loans pool rate which applied to other council borrowing. The 1980 Act changed this by requiring councils to charge the recommended building societies rate, or its own average loans pool rate plus a quarter per cent, whichever was the higher. So when society rates were below the council's pool rate plus 0.25 per cent, the society rates did not apply. When society rates were higher, councils had to charge building society rates, though there was no need for it – the worst of both worlds.

Not surprisingly, most council house sales were financed by the building societies and banks. Suddenly, with the steep rise in interest rates in 1989, councils found themselves charging 14.5 per cent on their mortgage loans, about 3-4 per cent more than is needed – average loans pool rates are mostly between 10 and 11 per cent. The damage and hardship which the system inflicts on those who chose a council mortgage, usually the less well off purchasers, is manifest.

The success of the right to buy – a million and a half sales so far – could not mask the fact that very large numbers of council tenants are unable to afford even a discounted mortgage. So ministers came up with another scheme to try to reduce the numbers continuing as tenants: 'rent to mortgage' is a scheme which enables tenants to become owners of a share of their home by converting their existing rent into a mortgage repayment. Pilot schemes were set up in Scotland, Wales, Milton Keynes and Basildon, Essex, and despite the very low level of take up compared with the interest in the right to buy, the government included rent to mortgage in the Leasehold Reform, Housing and Urban Development Act, 1993.

Under rent to mortgage tenants can buy a share of their house or flat, and the size of that share is calculated on the basis of the mortgage that can be supported from repayments equal to the current rent. At current interest rates (eight per cent) a rent of £35 a week converted into a mortgage repayment would service a loan of more than £20,000, thereby allowing tenants to buy 50-70 per cent of their home, depending on the part of the country. The maximum proportion that can be purchased is 80 per cent. Rent to mortgage purchasers are entitled to the same percentage discounts as right to buy purchasers but the discount is based on the proportion being purchased, not the full value of the property.

Rent to mortgage is different from conventional shared ownership in that purchasers do not continue to pay rent on the unpurchased proportion of the dwelling.

Financial effects of sales

If a sale is financed by a council mortgage loan, the council makes a saving on repairs costs, perhaps some saving on management costs, and receives interest on the outstanding loan. Against this it loses the rent and any housing subsidy payable.

There will also be an annual repayment of principal, very little in the early years, more in later years. But since this is a capital receipt it will not be credited to the housing revenue account. It will be applied to reducing the council's housing debt or be added to other housing capital receipts and used for capital spending or be invested.

Most sales, however, will be financed from some other source probably a building society. As with a council loan there will be savings on repairs and perhaps management and there will be a loss of rent income and subsidy where this was still payable. But because the council receives the whole of the sale price at once, there will be no annual mortgage repayments.

If the proceeds are invested, there will be investment income and this goes to the income side of the housing revenue account. If they are used for debt redemption, the loan charges falling on the HRA will be less. And if they are used for new capital expenditure, the HRA will benefit by having less loan charges to bear than if the council had borrowed to finance that capital expenditure.

Other effects of council house sales

There is no doubt about the advantages of the right to buy scheme for those who can afford to buy. For the council, however, the advantages of sales are a matter of some controversy. The selling price, even after the huge discount, will generally be much more than the outstanding debt on the house and it has therefore been argued that selling cannot fail to be profitable. This is like saying that someone who sells a house worth £50,000, bought long ago for £10,000 and with an outstanding mortgage loan of say £6,000, gains £14,000 by selling for £20,000 (£20,000 proceeds less outstanding loan £6,000, net proceeds £14,000). This is obvious nonsense. An asset worth £50,000 has been exchanged for £20,000 cash. The net proceeds are £14,000 when they ought to be £44,000. Whilst it is true that a great number of people have benefited financially from the right to buy, it is also true that some people who were induced into buying flats now find that their properties are virtually unsaleable and they are liable for very high service charges.

There are two even more important issues. First, there is the elementary question as to what sense there can be in selling houses so far below their real value that it will take several sales to provide one replacement of similar quality; and this at a time of such desperate scarcity of rented accommodation.

Second, the alleged profitability of such sales is an illusion. The immediate apparent gain – investment income on sale proceeds which exceeds rent income – is real enough the first year, but is less the year after by the amount by which the rent would have risen if the house had been retained. And less again the year after, and in a few years a cross-over point is reached and the gains turn into losses of ever greater magnitude.

A financial appraisal of the effects of sales was in fact produced for the Labour government in 1977 but not published. It came to light only because of its disclosure by *The Guardian*'s correspondent David Hencke some years later. It showed sales resulting in profits to councils in the earlier years when mortgage repayments exceeded what the rents would have been but turning into substantial losses in later years as rents continued to increase. A second paper, done for the new Conservative government in 1980 (presumably by the same civil servants, with admirable flexibility of mind) showed continuing profits. The different answer resulted from the different assumptions made in the second paper about future subsidies, costs, and rent increases.

A study, carried out for the House of Commons Environment Select Committee and published in 1981, found that some of the assumptions which enabled the second paper to portray sales as yielding a profit were totally unrealistic. It calculated that, in fact, the long term losses on council house sales, calculated over a 50 year period, were likely to average £12,500 per dwelling. On this basis the 1.5 million houses sold so far mean an eventual loss of £18.75 billion (at mid-1980s prices). Yet even these calculations did not allow for the enormous rent increases which have actually occurred since 1981.

Another sleight of hand by the DoE was its claim that it would generously allow councils to supplement their HIP allocations and so increase the amount they could spend on housing provision or improvement by letting them use part of the capital receipts which come from sales for capital spending. At first the DoE said 50 per cent, then 40 per cent, then 20 per cent.

Restrictions on the use of capital receipts in the 1980s resulted in a huge accumulation of receipts in local authority coffers, reaching £6 billion in the late 1980s. Meanwhile authorities saw their HIP allocations reduced year after year as the condition of their housing stocks declined. The money was there to tackle the problems of disrepair and modernisation but the government made it even more difficult to spend. The Local Government and Housing Act 1989 required authorities to use receipts to write off old debts rather than invest in better housing. This is discussed later.

Council housing after 1989

When the Conservatives won the 1987 election they could look back on the great strides they had made. Over a million council houses had passed into owner-occupation. Council building for rent had reduced sharply to an appalling 16,111 starts in 1988 while a million families remained on council waiting lists. Council building programmes suffered further cuts after 1989 and by 1992 completions were down to a derisory 4,085 in Great Britain as a whole.

Housing subsidies, £1,423 million in 1980-81, had been cut to £409 million in 1985-86. And those changes to the subsidy system resulted in massive rent increases, as intended.

But in the government's view, much still remained to be done, and a White Paper, *Housing: The Government's proposals* (Cm 214, September 1987), set out the next aims.

The proportion of owner-occupation in Britain, one of the highest in the world, was to be expanded. Housing associations, together with private and commercial landlords, were to be the future providers of rented housing. Private landlords would have freedom to charge market rents for new lettings.

Council housing still dominated the rented market; but in the government's view it was often not in the best interests of tenants. Although management was good in some places, it was distant and bureaucratic in the big cities, with poor maintenance performance in many areas. There was indiscriminate subsidy from the rates; and whole communities had slipped into permanent dependency on the welfare state. Local authorities should therefore cease to provide housing, and would have an 'enabling' role in encouraging other landlords to make provision.

The White Paper said that council tenants must have more opportunity to control their own destinies, including the right to choose other landlords. There were to be powers to set up housing action trusts to renovate run-down council housing in the inner cities.

Large Scale Voluntary Transfers

The proposals in the White Paper represented the most radical shake-up of rented housing in Britain with the potential to bring an early end to council housing as we had known it for 70 years. Some councillors and chief housing officers saw a threat to the continued supply of social rented housing in their areas and developed the idea of outflanking a piece-meal break-up of the stock by transferring the ownership of all their housing to newly established housing associations. Others came up with the same idea for very different reasons – a wish to get the council out of the business of providing housing. It is important to remember that the idea of large scale voluntary transfer (LSVT) was not a government proposal and that it was promoted by local authorities themselves – a good example of 'bottom up' policy making.

LSVT got off to a rather shaky start and the first few authorities to work up schemes failed to carry them through, largely because of opposition from tenants. But others learned from their experience and the first transfer took place in 1988 when Chiltern District Council in Buckinghamshire transferred its stock to the newly created Chiltern Hundreds Housing Association. By 1994 150,000 dwellings had been transferred in 32 local authority areas, although a roughly equal number had failed to go through. All but five of these transfers are in the south of England and East Anglia.

In financial terms LSVT is essentially a re-mortgaging exercise, much like a home-owner with a small mortgage in relation to the value of their property, who raises cash for improvements by taking out a new loan. In the case of council housing, this process requires a transfer of ownership but the principle is the same. LSVT is also a way of breaking out of the public expenditure conventions which have led to such severe limitations on local authority freedom to invest. One of the great advantages of LSVT is that the new association is not counted as part of the public sector and so it is free to raise loans for investment in improvements and new building. Another attraction to the local council is the prospect of a large capital receipt, as much as £117 million in the case of Bromley.

The way that LSVT works financially is that the stock to be transferred has to be valued, and the price paid by the new landlord is invariably well below the amount raised if the houses were sold individually under the right to buy. This is because the valuation takes into account the need to invest in repairs and improvements, the future rental income and the fact that transferring tenants retain their right to buy. The average transfer price has been around £8,800 per dwelling.

A factor which helped to make LSVT financially attractive was that housing associations, unlike local authorities, are not liable to have a proportion of their tenants' housing benefit entitlement netted off against notional surpluses (see the following section on the new financial regime for local authority housing). This meant that there was a significant additional cost falling on the Treasury as a result of transfer. The Treasury does not usually tolerate situations like this for long, and in 1993 the government introduced a levy of 20 per cent on any capital receipt arising from LSVT, as a way of recouping some of the extra housing benefit cost.

The new capital finance system

The changes in the 1987 white paper required a reform of housing finance, set out in two consultation papers issued in July 1988. One was called *Capital Expenditure and Finance* and covered other services as well as housing; the other, *New Financial Regime for Local Authority Housing*, dealt with the housing revenue account, subsidies, rents and housing finance generally.

The proposals in the White Paper were introduced in the Housing Act 1988. The financial reforms followed in the Local Government and Housing Act 1989 which came into force on 1 April 1990.

The system in operation until April 1990 controlled the capital expenditure of councils and prescribed what this was: mainly acquisition and development of land, building work, vehicles, plant and machinery, housing repairs when the cost is met by borrowing, and capital grants and advances. Expenditure was authorised by the annual Housing Investment Programme (HIP), and the allocation was normally backed by borrowing approval. Repair work which was not financed by borrowing did not count as 'prescribed expenditure'.

There was a ten per cent tolerance between years to allow for the carry-over of unspent allocations. Overspending was not illegal.

Capital receipts (mainly from the sale of council houses) could also be used, though only 20 per cent could be used for 'prescribed' expenditure (eg. for new building) in the year that the council received the money. Twenty per cent of any remaining receipts could be used the next year and so on. Thus over a period of years this 'cascade' effect permitted virtually the whole amount to be spent. In addition, councils could use receipts for 'non-prescribed' expenditure (this allowed them to renovate their existing stock). Local authorities made good use of their powers to use capital receipts – because they could build and repair without having to borrow (which would have used up scarce borrowing permission). The right to carry forward unspent capital receipts was seen by housing authorities as natural. It was their money arising from the sale of their property. But the government saw the cascade effect as a danger; they wanted the bulk of receipts to be used to pay off existing debts.

The new system introduced in 1990 therefore set out to control borrowing instead of expenditure. It applies to the financing of any capital expenditure not met from revenue and uses the term credit arrangement to cover borrowing and its equivalent. The definition of what constitutes capital expenditure is wider than before. For example, it includes 'enhancement' which is anything that substantially lengthens the life of an asset, increases its market value or increases the extent to which it can be used.

Each year the DoE issues to every housing authority its HIP allocation, which consists of an annual capital guideline (ACG) and an allocation of specified capital grants (SCG). The SCG refers to expenditure on private sector renovation through the improvement grant system and the ACG is broadly the amount available to be spent on the public sector stock. There are two further items to consider: when setting borrowing limits for each authority, the DoE specifies an amount of capital receipts taken into account (RTIA), which has the effect of reducing the permitted level of borrowing but then there are supplementary credit approvals (SCAs), which can be agreed by the DoE for specific purposes and which increase the level of permitted borrowing.

There is a fundamental change to the rules for the use of capital receipts. Only 25 per cent of receipts can be used for capital purposes. The remaining 75 per cent must be used to repay debt despite the fact that councils face gigantic problems of repair and modernisation and even though their housing debt is a tiny fraction of the current value of their property. There is about as much sense in this as there would be if a householder, faced with a leaking roof, were to use all his or her available cash to make a premature reduction in their outstanding mortgage.

Each council is issued with a single basic credit approval (BCA) for capital expenditure on all services in the coming year. This is the council's authority to meet capital expenditure by borrowing or credit arrangements. In fixing the BCA, the secretary of state can take account of the usable capital receipts belonging to that council, and so a council which is deemed to have a low need to spend and a high level of capital receipts can find itself with a BCA of zero. The BCA covers all council services and there is no ring fence around capital, so that councils can decide to use housing credit approvals and housing capital receipts for non-housing purposes and vice versa. However, in practice there is a limit to the amount that can be borrowed for housing because the DoE tells each authority the maximum level of loan charges eligible for Housing Revenue Account Subsidy each year. Borrowing approvals can only be used in the year to which they relate. Any unused allocation cannot be carried forward and any overspending will be deducted from the following year's BCA.

Some councils use revenue income to finance capital projects. There is no limit on the amount of capital expenditure which can be covered directly from revenue but the freedom is more cosmetic than actual. Any use of it will affect rent levels, since no support can be given from the general fund.

Supplementary credit approvals (SCA) may be issued at any time. Approvals for estate action schemes and other government initiatives are the sort of items which SCAs are used for.

Under the previous system, grants made by housing authorities for renovation or improvement were financed by borrowing with councils receiving annual government subsidy towards the cost of the loan charges on such borrowing. Under the 1990 Act system, subsidy is by a lump sum grant called a specified capital grant.

Leasing arrangements on property, plant, vehicles and other items, widely used by councils in recent years, are now brought within the capital control system. They must be taken into account when a council's aggregate credit limit (ACL) is calculated. This broadly consists of outstanding debt plus the council's credit arrangements. A council has no power to borrow if it would cause the ACL to be exceeded. The extent of 'credit cover' deemed to be used when a credit arrangement is entered into is the cost in the first and subsequent years, discounted by a formula determined by the secretary of state.

Besides all the constraints listed above, any borrowing must be from British-based lenders, unless there is consent to do otherwise.

The new housing revenue system in England and Wales

Ninety-five councils were still receiving general housing subsidy in 1987/88, and all councils received rent rebate subsidy which met almost the total cost of rent rebates. Some councils who were not getting housing subsidy, were nevertheless giving substantial help to the HRA from the rates, in some cases well above the amounts assumed in the calculation of the rate support grant. Others, who were receiving housing subsidy, were producing surpluses which they transferred to their general rate funds. And some managed to balance their HRAs with rate fund contributions which were less than the assessments on which they were receiving rate support grant. In other words, from the government's point of view, public expenditure was not necessarily going where it was most needed.

In addition, the financial arrangements had failed to cope with changing circumstances. Because councils borrow on a historic cost basis, the cost of borrowing is eroded by inflation. This applies to house purchasers too or anyone else who borrows in inflationary times. As a result, there was a growing tendency towards bigger surpluses in HRAs. The government concluded that, since the financing of new buildings by councils has been partly offset by surpluses on earlier, low-cost building, a smaller building programme by councils in the future could create further surpluses.

HRA Surpluses Defined

'A STIMULUS FOR INVESTMENT'

'A CUSHION FOR INEFFICIENCY'

It therefore believed that these surpluses should not be available as a cushion for bad practice and inefficiency. The government's view was that while rents should not exceed levels within the reach of people in low paid employment and that they could be expected frequently to be below market levels, they should be set by reference to two parameters – what people can pay and what the property is worth – rather than by reference to historic cost.

The current revenue finance system is clearly a development from the system introduced by the 1980 Act but it differs from it in certain crucial ways. First, the HRA now has just one source of subsidy, known as the HRA subsidy, replacing what had previously been three quite separate and distinct forms of assistance: general subsidy, rent rebate subsidy and rate fund contributions. The effect of this move was to greatly expand what counted as the deficit on the HRA, thus returning virtually all authorities to the position where they were vulnerable to pressure to raise rents from subsidy withdrawal. The HRA subsidy consists of two elements, the rent rebate element (which is always a positive amount) and the housing element (which can be a negative amount). Thus:

HRA subsidy = Rebate element + or – Housing element.

Second, the HRA is ring-fenced, so that councils cannot keep rents low by drawing on their council tax income but nor can they keep the council tax low by creaming off surpluses from the HRA.

Third, whereas under the old system the determinations for rent increases and management and maintenance (M&M) allowances were the same for all authorities, under the system in the 1990 Act each authority gets its own guideline rent and M&M allowance each year.

Rent increases

The approach to rent setting in the 1990 Act is based on progress towards rents which, while having regard to what people can pay, are also related to what the property is worth. It is important to be clear that this is not the same as capital value rents, i.e. rents set at, say four per cent of the capital value; the government's approach is to say only that rent *increases* should reflect differences in capital values. This involves assessing the capital value of the housing stock of each council, using right to buy sale values (before discount). From this, the total value of all council housing in the country is derived. Each authority's stock is expressed as a proportion of the total national value. If a council owned a housing stock worth one per cent of the total then it would be expected to raise one per cent of the total rent income.

Each year the government decides what overall national increase it wants to see for the coming year and this overall figure is then divided amongst the various housing authorities according to their share of the total value. It is an odd way of doing things. With the vast difference in house prices across the country it soon became clear that it was producing some odd results. For example, the formula suggested that rents in the London Borough of Hillingdon would need to increase by 65 per cent. But Blackburn rents should be reduced by 51 per cent.

The government was obviously not going to accept that rents should go down anywhere and a system of 'damping' was introduced so as to ensure that rents everywhere continued to rise but not by amounts that were unacceptably high in political terms. Table 3 shows the range of guideline increases since 1990/91.

Table 3   Guideline Rent Increases in England, 1990/91–1994/95

Guideline increases	1990/91	1991/92	1992/93	1993/94	1994/95
Minimum	£0.95	£1.38	£1.20	£1.50	£1.50
Maximum	£4.50	£2.50	£4.50	£3.00	£2.90

The £4.50 maximum in 1990/91 was a very large increase when £2.95 had been the highest 'guideline' figure in the preceding ten years. But the new financial regime also allowed authorities to increase rents even further. The London Borough of Redbridge, for instance, increased rents in April 1990 by £15.64 a week (a 44 per cent increase) instead of the guideline 95p, Canterbury £12.29 (a 54 per cent increase), guideline £1.92, Bournemouth £9.00 (a 33 per cent increase), guideline £1.32.

Some authorities have continued to raise rents much faster than their guideline amounts. Rents generally have tended to rise by more than the guidelines even though the government has pursued a consistent policy of raising guidelines by around five per cent more than inflation. By 1993/94 the average council rent in England was £32.87 or almost 12 per cent above the average guideline. Average rents rose 33 per cent in real terms in the first four years of the system.

Council rents have risen by more than the guideline amounts for two main reasons. First, authorities have chosen to raise rents in order to pay for levels of management and maintenance above the DoE allowances, and second, they have funded an increased proportion of capital expenditure from revenue.

It is also important to note that rent increases have been greater in some regions than others because of the government's policy of relating guideline increases to property values. This has meant that most authorities in the north have had the minimum guideline increase each year, amounting to only £6.53 in five years, compared with the cumulative figure of £16.40 for those authorities (mostly in the south) given the maximum guideline increase each year.

Management and maintenance

Management and maintenance allowances are crucial to the way the system works. The DoE makes assumptions about management and maintenance expenditure in each local authority area, and in the first year, 1990/91, they merely rolled forward the old system and gave authorities an eight per cent increase. Since 1991/92, however, M&M allowances have been based on information about the characteristics of the stock in each area. This is not to say that allowances are based on a view of what particular authorities need to spend on their housing; instead the information on the stock is used as a way of dividing up the total amount that the Treasury has agreed should be available for M&M allowances. The idea is to target larger increases in allowances on those authorities deemed to be underspending according to the formula.

In 1991/92 the total increase was six per cent but with inflation also assumed to be six per cent there was no increase in real terms, and authorities that were to be encouraged to spend more could only benefit from targeting if others received allowances increased by less than six per cent. In that year 44 authorities benefited, at the expense of 36 high spending authorities, whose allowances were frozen at their 1990/91 levels, and all the rest whose allowances increased by a little less than inflation.

The following year the total allowance was increased by 6.5 per cent in cash, which was seen as a two per cent increase in real terms. This time all authorities in England received at least 3.5 per cent extra in cash, while 135 benefited from targeting. In 1993/94 there was a real increase of one per cent in the total amount, over 57 per cent of English authorities received a nil cash increase in order to pay for targeting. In 1994/95 the total allowance was increased by four per cent (1.5 per cent in real terms), and again many authorities received nil cash increases to pay for targeting.

Many councils have criticised the government for the low levels of increase in M&M allowances, partly because of the lack of scope for service improvements and partly because of the effect of new restrictions on capital expenditure brought in under the 1989 Act. The previously widespread practice of borrowing or using capital receipts to meet the cost of major repairs was seriously restricted under the new capital system. The choice for many councils is therefore to cut repairs programmes or further increase rents.

How the system works

The 1989 Act meant a massive transfer of power to central government to make virtually all meaningful decisions about council housing – on rent levels, on expenditure on maintenance, improvement and rehabilitation, and on management.

By combining rent rebate subsidy with general housing subsidy, the DoE ensures that nearly every housing authority, at least for the present, is entitled to HRA subsidy. But already, by 1994/95 in three quarters of housing authorities in England the general subsidy element of HRA subsidy is negative. This means that the HRA subsidy received is composed entirely of the rent rebate element, and that the negative housing element is netted off against the rebate element, as explained earlier (page 40). In other words, those tenants who pay the full rent are in effect contributing towards the cost of the housing benefit claimed by their less well off neighbours.

Figures in the *DoE Annual Report 1994* show that for the first time in 1993/94 the total of negative housing subsidy entitlements in England exceed the total of positive entitlements, to the tune of £66million. Council housing has reached the point where, in overall terms, the national HRA is no longer in subsidy, and the surplus is projected to rise to a massive £688million by 1996/97, by which time council tenants paying rent will be bearing 28 per cent of the cost of housing benefit for other council tenants.

Despite the growing number of authorities with a negative housing subsidy entitlement, the great majority are still receiving some HRA subsidy. This leaves them subject to DoE leverage on rent levels. Leverage is at the heart of the system and it is important to note the comparisons between the rate of guideline rent increases and the changes in M&M allowances. In each year since the system started the DoE has raised the guideline rents by more than the M&M allowances. The greater the difference between the two figures, the greater is the withdrawal of subsidy and the greater the pressure on councils to raise their rents.

The DoE points out, however, that councils have freedom to determine rents; and this is true, so long as they produce the specified rent income. Indeed, they even have freedom to set rents which produce less than the specified rent income; so long as they reduce expenditure which offsets the reduced rent income.

It is the same with expenditure. Councils are free to spend above DoE criteria, as long as they increase rents still further, to cover the overspending. If there is a deficit, this must be carried forward and budgeted for, in the following year.

Council rents increased by a massive 423 per cent in cash terms, or 98 per cent in real terms between 1979 and 1993. One third of the real terms increase occurred after the introduction of the 1989 Act system as the government has pressed ahead with its plan to force public sector rents closer to those in the profit driven private sector. But what is the point of ever higher council rents when the majority of tenants rely on housing benefit and many of the rest are on low wages?

Workers in service industries, pensioners and people with low incomes, usually have earnings based on national scales; and when they do not, their incomes will certainly bear little relationship to the huge variations in property prices in different areas. For these people, who make up the bulk of council tenants, council housing, with its minimal variations in rent levels in the various regions, has been a blessing. The South East region, the most

expensive in England (apart from London), had unrebated rents in 1993/94 which averaged £38.79. The least expensive were Yorkshire and Humberside (£25.91) and the Northern region (£27.54). The rest were in between (*ADC/AMA Housing Finance Survey 1993/94*).

But average house prices ranged from £72,243 in the Outer Metropolitan area around London and £58,037 in the outer South East down to £42,422 in Yorkshire and Humberside (*Nationwide Building Society House Prices Bulletin*, 4th Quarter of 1993). What possible justification can there be for attempting to relate rent levels to this? And if we do, what becomes of labour mobility?

All this arises from the absurd ideological dogma which argues that unless rents represent a return on current values, the tenant is being subsidised even if he or she is paying more than the cost of providing and maintaining the accommodation.

This selective vision ignores the subsidising of house purchase by mortgage interest tax relief – that remarkable system which gives help whether there is need or not.

Yet the government seems set on its course. The outlook in the coming years is that council rents will go on rising, the proportion of tenants who need rebates will rise further as will the total cost of rebates. The government will then find itself attempting to shift that large and growing burden onto a diminishing proportion of tenants who are not eligible for rebates.

This is the most discreditable of the 'reforms' in the 1989 Act. There is no intention of treating housing associations in this fashion, and even to think of trying to do so to private landlords would be ludicrous.

Meanwhile, waiting lists will lengthen and the scandal and economic folly of homelessness will go on increasing, for nothing effective is proposed to deal with the basic cause – the shortage of rented accommodation.

The costs of homelessness

It is impossible to be precise about the costs of homelessness. How can a monetary value be placed on broken relationships, ruined childhoods and lost job opportunities? One thing we can be certain of is that the cost of homelessness in this wider sense is far greater than the financial expenditure involved. In terms of public expenditure, all the money spent by councils and most of that spent by housing associations on the provision of homes is about the prevention or relief of homelessness.

However, homelessness is only one factor, and a relatively minor one at that, in the formula used by the DoE to distribute capital spending allocations. In November 1989 the secretary of state announced a two year package of £250 million for additional help for the homeless, although conditions attached to the deal made it clear that councils had to channel resources into housing association provision and that they themselves were not going to be able to build new houses.

This package followed a period during which homelessness had been increasing rapidly and the government had appeared to be uninterested in the problem. The 1987 White Paper on housing failed to mention homelessness, yet between 1978 and 1992 there was a 180 per cent increase in the numbers of homeless households accepted by local authorities in England. The total for England in 1993 was no fewer than 139,790. During the late 1980s and early 1990s the number of homeless households in temporary accommodation increased rapidly, exceeding 52,690 at the beginning of 1994. However, the use of the least suitable form of temporary accommodation, bed and breakfast hotels, declined as more authorities developed private sector leasing schemes.

By 1990, the government's concern had grown to the extent of two further measures to try to reduce the visible presence of the homeless on the street. The first was an increase in the support given to voluntary housing aid and advice agencies (costing £6.45 million in 1993/94) and the second was the announcement in June 1990 of a package designed to get single homeless people off the streets of London. In its first three years the Rough Sleepers Initiative channelled over £96 million to housing associations and voluntary organisations helping single homeless people and the total is set to rise to £182 million by 1995/96, according to the *DoE Annual Report 1994*.

These sums need to be set alongside the amounts spent each year by local authorities in providing for homeless people under the terms of Part 111 of the Housing Act, 1985. In 1992/93 CIPFA statistics (based on 334 authorities in England and Wales) show that total net expenditure on homelessness was £196 million, of which £123.8 million (63.2%) was spent by London councils.

A quarter of this sum, £49 million, was spent on bed and breakfast accommodation. B&B hotels are both highly unsatisfactory for homeless people and hugely expensive for local councils. The (gross) cost of keeping a family in bed and breakfast for a year is £12,200, while the estimated first year of rehousing them in a new council house would only be £7,000 (*Homes Cost Less Than Homelessness, Shelter 1992*).

3 Housing Associations

Long before councils became involved in the provision of rented housing, there were housing associations, usually established with the aid of charitable money from wealthy benefactors, providing dwellings at modest rents. The Peabody, Guinness, and Sutton Dwelling Trust are three well-known examples.

The movement spread and eventually government subsidies similar to those paid to councils became available. New kinds of organisations were tried – cost-rent, co-ownership, co-operative, self-build; but by far the major provision was still of dwellings for rent for those in need. However, the total stock, some 250,000 dwellings by 1970, was still small compared to the five million or so then provided by councils.

The 1970-74 Conservative government decided upon a great expansion of the housing association movement as a supplement (or perhaps as an alternative) to council housing. The Housing Corporation, set up in 1964 to encourage the formation of cost-rent and co-ownership societies, was chosen as the main agent for encouraging the formation of housing associations to provide accommodation at fair rents. The Corporation would have an important supervisory function: it would examine and approve schemes, and the government would provide the necessary financial support.

A Bill to provide the relevant powers was drafted but before it reached the statute book, the 1974 Labour government had come into office. It promptly took over the previous government's measure without alteration. With the Housing Act 1974, the great expansion began.

The movement had already been growing and Shelter had played a notable part in that growth, raising some £3 million by national appeals in 1969 and 1970, which it used mainly to start housing associations in areas of severe housing stress and so supplement the work of the local authorities. By

1971, the associations were providing an extra 10,000 dwellings a year, a big increase on anything they had managed previously. But with the impetus given by the financial arrangements of the 1974 Act and the work of the Housing Corporation, this more than trebled by 1976 with 35,300 completions. Since then, however, there have been dramatic cuts in public expenditure and some diversion of resources to conversion for sale. Annual completions during the 1980s never exceeded 16,600 and by 1986 had fallen to 12,571.

Yet the associations have widened the choice open to would-be tenants and this has been especially important because some associations have displayed a willingness to house groups who have, in the past, been excluded from council accommodation. It has to be admitted that councils have often had an understandable, but possibly excessive, preference for 'looking after their own'.

Finance for the great expansion

The dramatic progress from 1974 onwards resulted from a new subsidy system, though the word 'subsidy' was tactfully avoided. From then on it was 'capital grants' or housing association grant (HAG). Previously, when subsidies were given, they had been annual ones, as in the local authority sector, to meet part of the running costs. Now they were once-for-all lump sum grants which met most of the capital cost immediately. With these went a new rent system, 'fair rents', set by rent officers, as in the private sector.

The starting point for the new system was the rent which the rent officer recommended. The likely annual costs of management and maintenance, which would be the first call on the rent income, were then estimated. What was left after meeting those costs would be available for meeting loan charges on any money borrowed. It would not be very much and would service a loan which would meet only a small proportion of the total capital cost of providing the dwellings. The rest, the major part of the capital cost, was met by an outright capital grant (HAG).

Suppose, for example, that the total cost of provision for a house outside London was £10,000 in 1975:

Table 4 How HAG was Calculated, pre-1989

	£ per annum
Fair rent @ £9 per week	470
Management & Maintenance Allowance	150
Amount available for loan charges	320
This would cover loan charges on a loan of approximately	2320
Therefore HAG would be	7680
	10,000

The grant in this example meant a payment of about 77 per cent of the total cost of provision, remarkably generous compared with previous systems. The associations were scarcely able to believe their good fortune. But this special treatment was needed for associations to expand, since they did not have the great advantage, which councils had, of a large stock of earlier built low-cost housing which, by rent pooling, kept average rent levels down.

The enthusiasm of many councils for the new scheme was limited as they compared it with their own subsidy scheme but they welcomed the greater variety and freedom of choice for tenants. The enthusiasm of the Treasury was likewise restrained, for the immediate cost was very heavy. Yet that large once-for-all subsidy in 1975, £7,680 in the example quoted, had produced a dwelling which must now be worth over £50,000, with a mere £2,000 or so outstanding loan debt. A remarkable bargain, by any standards.

Of course, by 1989 there had been a dramatic change. The rent which a rent officer would set had trebled and the cost of provision had more than trebled. Inevitably, the cost of subsidising had risen steeply, to 80 or 90 per cent of a much higher cost of provision, hence the government's growing concern and the new financial arrangements from April 1989, described later.

There was a minor problem which the new system got over without difficulty. Development and other preliminary costs – land purchase, payments to the builder – have to be met before the rents begin to come in or the grant is finally settled. The Housing Corporation resolved this by providing temporary loans, the interest on which was treated as part of the overall cost of provision.

There could also be a second subsidy, a 'revenue deficit grant'. Because of controls on rents, associations could find themselves in deficit on the revenue account. A case could then be made to the DoE for grant assistance on the year's operations. The grant would not be a continuing one unless the need could be shown to persist.

There was one astonishing oversight in the 1974 Act. We live in inflationary times, and rents rise significantly at regular intervals. A capital grant (HAG) which was appropriate when the grant was given would be too generous a few years later when the rents had gone up substantially after several rent reviews. A scheme which broke even at first would soon be making a surplus. Yet the subsidy had all been given in one lump sum. It could not, like an annual subsidy, be reduced in future years when the need was less.

The light eventually dawned on the DoE and the Housing Act 1980 required associations to keep a 'grant redemption fund' (GRF) into which surpluses on HAG-aided schemes were paid. The DoE could thus get some of its money back, or require surpluses to be used, for instance, for major repairs which otherwise would require grant aid.

Table 5 Council Rents Versus Fair Rents

	Average council rents, England & Wales	Average fair rent for Housing Associations	Percentage difference
	£	£	%
1978	5.85	10.08	72.3
1979	6.40	10.69	67.0
1980	7.71	12.52	62.4
1981	11.43	13.96	22.1
1982	13.50	15.62	15.7
1983	14.00	17.15	22.5
1984	14.71	18.65	26.8
1985	15.59	19.69	26.3
1986	16.41	21.42	30.5
1987	17.24	22.85	32.5
1988	18.74	24.75	32.1
1989	20.64	26.65	29.1

Source: Housing and Construction Statistics 1977-87 and 1990, DoE, and CIPFA Council Rents at April 1989

Rents before the 1988 Act

The fair rents which housing associations charged as a condition of receiving HAG were generally higher than for comparable council dwellings. The difference narrowed as the 1980 Act produced drastic rent increases for council housing but widened again as council rent increases slowed down as housing subsidies were reduced until they ceased altogether for most councils outside London. As this happened the DoE lost much of its leverage for forcing rent increases on unwilling councils, and in the meantime, fair rents were continuing their uninterrupted upward course (see Table 5).

Sales

The 'right to buy' scheme under the Housing Act 1980, as it applies to council tenants, is described in the chapter on council housing. The government wanted to extend the scheme to housing associations but they objected strongly. They saw no justification for being compelled to sell off their stock when their very reason for existence was to own houses which could be let at modest rents. Most associations were registered charities which raised legal and moral problems with sales. The House of Lords agreed with this and the government gave way. The right to buy was confined to tenants of non-charitable associations. In the case of charitable associations the government settled for giving them the power to sell if they so chose. Even then, the power would not apply where it was in conflict with the terms of an association's trust. Where associations did sell, the discounts were the same as for council dwellings sold.

Between 1980 and 1984, only 5,309 association houses were sold, about one per cent of the total stock. (In the same period council house sales were 625,775, about ten per cent of the stock).

The government tried again. The Housing and Building Control Bill 1984 proposed to extend the sales scheme to all dwellings owned by charitable housing associations. Again, some pressure in the Commons, and very considerable pressure in the Lords, obliged the government to drop the proposal.

Instead it introduced a scheme for portable discounts called HOTCHA (Home-Ownership for Tenants of Charitable Housing Associations). Tenants, whose association refused to agree a voluntary sale at a discount, could apply for a grant equivalent to what the discount would have been if the association had been willing to sell. The grant had to be used to assist the purchase of a house on the open market. Only associations nominated by the Housing Corporation could operate the scheme, and in its first year only 31 associations (out of over 2,000) were nominated, and only 159 actual sales were completed.

The government withdrew the HOTCHA scheme in 1988, and launched a replacement for it in 1990. The Tenants Incentive Scheme (TIS) is similarly aimed at spreading home-ownersship and it operates by giving tenants cash grants to enable them to move into the owner-occupier market. The government plans to encourage greater use of TIS, with a programme of 7,000 grants each year up to 1996/97.

In addition to TIS, the government has reintroduced Do It Yourself Shared Ownership (DIYSO) which was originally launched in 1983. Both TIS and DIYSO are schemes for encouraging housing association tenants to move out and generate vacancies in the rented stock but under DIYSO the tenant continues to rent half their new home and to pay a mortgage on the other half. DIYSO works on the basis that tenants wishing to move find themselves a suitable house (within specified price limits – which vary from place to place) and their housing association buys the house. The tenant then pays rent based on half the value and makes mortgage repayments on the other half. In 1992/93 the DIYSO programme amounted to 4,500 units and is expected to grow.

The Housing Act 1988

In its 1987 White Paper, the government saw the housing association movement as the standard bearer for the provision of rented housing. Councils would be 'enablers', not providers; future provision would be the task of housing associations and private landlords (described as the 'independent rented sector').

This future provision was to be funded by a much higher element of private finance. However, the associations had been heavily dependent on Exchequer support, typically capital grants of 80-90 per cent of the cost of provision because fair rents had covered only a small proportion of their costs. So assured tenancies were required when associations provided new dwellings, or re-let existing dwellings, to allow them to charge higher rents to service privately raised loans. Associated with this was the need to remove controls on rents in order to attract private finance.

The legal framework for the new arrangements was provided in the Housing Act 1988. Since changes in the grant structure do not require legislation (the Secretary of State has the necessary powers), the provisions of the Act, insofar as they affect housing associations, dealt with the introduction of assured and assured shorthold forms of tenancy, security of tenure, rights of succession, and other matters which arise from the changeover from the fair rents system. The Housing Corporation continues to supervise associations in England. It has wide powers to determine grant levels and procedures. New bodies, Tai Cymru (Housing for Wales), and Scottish Homes (a merger of the Scottish Special Housing Association and the Housing Corporation in Scotland) have taken on the Housing Corporation's responsibilities there.

The new regime

From 1 April 1989, there have been far-reaching changes to virtually all the arrangements for providing future housing association dwellings and the financial management of the existing stock. The new system is based on the premise that the more private finance that is available, the greater will be the provision of rented housing, as limited public finance will be stretched further. It is also based on the premise that associations should carry the risk attached to the use of private loans – the old system had been virtually risk free for associations.

The system, therefore, provides that although HAG continues to be available, its average proportion of the cost of new build or rehabilitation is less than before. The remaining amount which needs to be borrowed (and which all used to count as public expenditure because it came from the Housing Corporation or the local authority), is mostly provided from private finance under 'mixed funding' arrangements.

Under the old HAG system, the amount of grant depended on what the fair rent would be and the cost of each individual scheme. The government's current approach reverses this procedure by taking the cost of provision as the starting point and avoiding the considerable amount of detailed work that used to fall on the Housing Corporation by assessing grant rates based on tables of costs in eight geographical areas, for ten different sizes of dwelling and for four categories of provision – new build, rehabilitation, and two groups of special provision. For example, the all-in cost of an 80 square metre three to five person dwelling in Group A (the most expensive) in 1994/95 is £87,800; in Group F (the cheapest) it is £55,900.

The overall average level of HAG has fallen fast under the new regime, from 75 per cent in 1989/90 to 62 per cent in 1994/95, with the prospect of 55 per cent in 1995/96. It is important to note that these are average figures which mask wide regional variations – some associations already work with

HAG rates below 55 per cent.

When private finance was first mooted there was talk of 30 per cent public, 70 per cent private funding, to produce twice or three times as many houses as under the old system. There was a rapid change of mind when it was realised what this would mean in terms of rent levels and a 50/50 sharing was indicated. Finally, in December 1988, as the consequences of a 50/50 system dawned, it was announced that there would be a public funding average of 75 per cent with no upper limit.

The funding framework

There are now two main types of funding – 'mixed', with HAG from public sources and the rest raised from private sources; and 'public' where HAG comes from the Housing Corporation and the rest, the loans, comes either from the Housing Corporation or the local authority.

Associations capable of raising private loans must do so. Many, however, are too small or not able for other reasons to do this and have to look, as before, to the local council or the Housing Corporation.

The financing of developments is also divided into three other groups 'cash programme' (previously referred to as 'tariff'), 'non-tariff mixed funding' and 'non-tariff public funding'. Cash programme funding is for financially strong associations which can raise private finance for new capital projects. They submit a three year programme of development not individual scheme applications. The association negotiates an agreement with each regional office of the Housing Corporation in whose area it proposes to build housing. The agreement will define areas, housing need, numbers and types of dwellings, and the grant payable during the three years. Once set, the agreement and the rate per unit will not be amended and there is no individual scheme scrutiny. Cash programme status has many advantages for associations, but it is to be withdrawn from April 1995.

Non-tariff mixed funding is for associations which are expected to use mixed funding but are not suitable in terms of size, reserves and so on for tariff funding. There is assessment of individual schemes. There is also some limited allowance for cost variation after approval. Costs can rise while the work is under way, so this can be allowed for at the final assessment. There is less risk here for an association than in cash programme funding but any excess cost over the above limit will have to be met by the association.

Non-tariff public funding applies to associations unlikely to attract private finance such as those catering for special needs or providing hostels. The procedure is the same as for non-tariff mixed funding apart from some additional scrutiny at project approval stage to cover planning, land valuation and minor matters.

The capital programme

In 1988/89, the last year of the old regime, housing associations had a capital programme of £568 million. There was then a huge increase over the next four years so that by 1992/93 the total was £2,300 million, to which must be added £626 million of private finance. The associations not only had to gear up to spend this much increased amount of money, they also had to come to terms with the mysteries of private finance. It is important to remember that until the late 1980s housing associations had not had to get involved with the business of raising development finance from private investors. Since then they have been on a steep learning curve, and management committees have had to acquire an understanding of a new and difficult area of decision making. By 1994 associations had raised over £2,600 million in private finance.

One reason for the very large capital programme in 1992/93 was the Housing Market Package (HMP) which was launched by the Chancellor in November 1992. This was a desperate attempt by the government to mop up unsold privately owned houses and thereby to put some life back into the deeply depressed housing market. Selected associations (81 in all) were given just 93 working days to spend £577 million (plus £328 million of private finance) but they managed it and bought over 18,000 houses. The injection of public expenditure in the HMP was not additional money but represented funds brought forward from future years. The effect, therefore, was to give associations a hectic time during the winter of 1992/93 but leaving them with less money to spend on the conventional, planned programme in the following period.

The impact of the new regime was that housing association output doubled between 1988 and 1992, reaching 25,640 dwellings across Great Britain. And in 1993 the total rose to 34,492.

'Affordable' rents

Affordability has been one of the big issues for housing associations in the 1990s. Until 1989 they did not have to worry about rent levels because these were set externally by the independent rent officer service. However, now associations have to set their own rents on all new lettings (both new build and relets of existing stock). They have had to do this in circumstances where the government has said that rents should remain affordable for people in low paid work while at the same time it has introduced a series of measures (specifically the use of private finance and lower grant rates) which have had the effect of putting strong upward pressure on rents.

For tenants who were in their homes before the new system started in 1989, their tenancies continue to be secure with fair rents set by the rent officer. Fair rents are reviewed every two years.

For properties provided under the new regime, associations are expected to set rents which cover costs while still being affordable for tenants on low incomes. Affordability is the term used by the government, but Ministers and the Housing Corporation have steadfastly refused to give a clear definition (although Sir George Young, the Housing Minister, in 1993 did let slip in evidence to the Select Committee on the Environment, that the DoE takes 35 per cent of net income to be an affordable level of expenditure on rent). This is of course a problem for the associations and as a result there has been considerable debate about the best way to define affordability.

The National Federation of Housing Associations has been very active on the issue of affordability and has produced a regularly updated table of 'indicative rents' for all the ten sizes of dwelling and all the geographical areas for which the cost tables cater. Initially the NFHA took 20 per cent as the affordable level but it moved on to 22 per cent and in 1993 adopted a new policy:

> Rents are affordable if the majority of working households taking up new tenancies are not caught in the poverty trap (because of dependency on housing benefit) or paying more than 25% of their net income on rent.
>
> (Housing Associations Weekly, 21 January 1994)

Indicator rents in mid-1994 calculated on this basis range from £49.89 a week for an 80 square metre, three to five person house in area A (the most costly) to £38.29 in area F (the least costly). Actual rents as monitored by the NFHA's CORE (continous recording) system had already reached £70.10 per week for three bed newly let assured tenancies in London in mid-1993, and £46.08 per week in Merseyside. In overall terms rents have increased rapidly since 1988, at rates faster than prices and incomes, and the gap between actual rents and the NFHA affordability measure has widened year by year.

By the middle of 1993 over 70 per cent of new assured tenants were paying rents above the affordable level, as defined in the new NFHA policy.

The rent surplus fund

There was, under the previous arrangements, the requirement to keep a grant redemption fund (GRF). This is now abolished. Instead each association must keep a rent surplus fund (RSF) which is different in important respects from the previous GRF.

The RSF arrangements do not apply to dwellings provided under the new HAG regime. RSF rules apply, only to old HAG schemes with their fair rents, where these are still charged, and the usually higher rents of houses re-let as assured tenancies. Gross rent income is calculated on the fair rents and, for re-lets, the higher of the actual rents is charged or the association's average fair rents. From this gross rent income, a four per cent allowance for voids and bad debts is deducted; loan charges; management and maintenance expenditure; service charges; miscellaneous items; rent losses which can arise when a new HAG dwelling is occupied by a tenant who retains security and fair rent rights.

From the net income thus calculated, the association must transfer 80 per cent to a sinking fund to meet the cost of future major repairs while the remaining 20 per cent is available to be used at the discretion of the association.

The outlook

Until the 1987 White Paper the housing association movement was seen by most people (including the DoE statistics section) as part of the public rented sector; and indeed it was more dependent on public funding than council housing. Like councils, it saw its purpose to provide for people who needed, or preferred, to rent, and its tenants have been as much in need of support from housing benefit as have council tenants.

It was regarded as the voluntary movement at its best: non-profit making; motivated by social considerations; an admirable supplement to council housing; making a particularly valuable contribution to special categories such as the elderly and the single homeless; and widening choices for would-be tenants. Since the 1988 Act, housing associations have had to come to terms with a very different set of pressures. They have had to devise their own rent setting policies for the first time; they have had to learn about private finance, and to live with the risks involved; they have had to do this at a time of rapid expansion in their capital programmes; and they have had to learn to be competitive with each other, in ways that many associations find quite alien to their traditions.

At first it seemed that the movement was set fair for continued long term growth but real doubts have now emerged. A combination of factors has soured the outlook for associations. The government's attempts to reduce its borrowing requirement, and to push housing associations ever further into the world of big business, led to continuing reductions in the grant rate. This has had serious consequences for rents. As grant rates fall, rents inevitably have to rise and this has a knock on effect on the total housing benefit bill – so the public expenditure savings are reduced.

Added to this has been the impact of the Page report (*Building for Communities*, 1993); David Page argued that the effect of the new financial system was to push associations into building larger estates, at higher densities, and to fill them with high proportions of households on very low incomes. He warned of the danger of reproducing the sorts of problems associated with the most rundown parts of the council sector. This was then seized on by some Conservative backbench MPs who also accused housing associations of undermining their majorities by moving non-Tory voting people into their areas. Some right wing Tory MPs have always seen housing associations as an undesirable force because they are neither democratically accountable (like local authorities) nor fully exposed to the realities of market forces (like private businesses).

It must be said that some housing associations have not helped the cause – they have been prepared to bid for development schemes at low grant rates thereby undermining claims that lower grant rates were not sustainable. If such schemes are produced to lower standards of design and specification and at higher densities, then the short-term advantage of growth will be gained at the expense of the tarnished reputation of the movement and the diminished circumstances of the people who have to live on these estates.

Having briefly been very much the flavour of the month with the government, housing associations now face a much more uncertain future. There are real dangers that the grant rate will be squeezed further and possibly eliminated altogether. Then associations will face some very difficult choices – about whether to stop developing new housing or to retain some development capacity by merging with other associations.

4 The Private Rented Sector

At the outbreak of the first world war, renting was the normal tenure. It accounted for 90 per cent of the housing stock, with only ten per cent owner-occupied, a tiny amount of housing association dwellings, and virtually no council houses. By 1992 private renting in Great Britain had shrunk to 9.5 per cent, declining every year as privately rented dwellings were sold for owner-occupation or became unfit, although there are claims that the decline has now come to a halt and that there are signs of growth. However, it is too early to say whether this is a temporary effect of the recession in the owner-occupier market.

Almost 60 per cent of private rented housing was built before the First World War and much of it has suffered from chronic neglect for a very long time. Figures from the latest round of house condition surveys in the different parts of Britain indicate that by far the worst conditions are found in the private rented sector, where rates of unfitness are typically three or four times greater than the average for the whole stock. Just over 16 per cent of private rented housing in Great Britain was found to be unfit and almost 27 per cent required urgent repairs costing more than £1000.

This is a shocking state of affairs and the reasons – largely financial – make a tangled and discreditable story.

In 1915, rents were frozen as a temporary war-time measure and tenants could not be evicted. But tenants were many and they all had votes and landlords were few. What began as a temporary measure became a permanent feature of housing policy. Other countries had imposed rent control but none behaved as ineptly as Britain which neither compensated landlords for lost income nor allowed rents to rise as incomes rose. Building for rent was already tailing off before 1914; other more attractive fields for investment had appeared. Rent control, in the rigid form it took, ensured that no sensible

63

investor would put money into rented housing: and no landlord, when a property became vacant, would think of re-letting if they could sell. If the intention had been to destroy the private rented sector, no more effective strategy could have been devised.

This folly continued for over 40 years, with only quite inadequate rent increases allowed at long intervals, until in 1957 the Conservative government grasped the nettle. The Rent Act 1957 removed controls on dwellings above certain rateable values and on any property (whatever the rateable value) when a tenant left. This, it was claimed, would halt the decline of the private rented sector by giving landlords a fair return on their investment.

The government appeared to have completely overlooked that in conditions of serious scarcity, de-control would open the door to widespread exploitation, and a new word, 'Rachmanism', came into the English language as a result of the activities of one of the more unscrupulous operators in this

field. Moreover, instead of stabilising, the sector began to decline faster than ever. As well as giving freedom to increase rents, de-control ended the tenant's security of tenure so a landlord could get rid of a tenant and sell with vacant possession. This was a much more attractive proposition than re-letting, even at a high rent. Besides, might not some misguided future government reimpose control?

And this is exactly what happened.

Fair rents

Even before the Conservatives lost the 1964 election, they had become alarmed at the effects of the Rent Act 1957 and had set up the Milner Holland Committee to examine the Greater London housing problem; and they would have had to do something about it if they had been returned to office.

As soon as the new Labour government took office, it moved swiftly with a temporary holding measure restoring security of tenure and freezing existing rents. When the Milner Holland Committee report appeared in 1965, the government lost no time. The Minister concerned was Richard Crossman and his problem was that he could not simply return to the old controlled rents which were quite inadequate. Nor could he, in conditions of desperate scarcity, leave rents to market forces.

So he devised 'fair rents', a novel and entirely artificial concept. The Rent Act 1965 did not define a 'fair' rent but where landlord and tenant could not agree on the rent level, a rent officer, appointed by the local authority, would decide what a fair rent should be.

In this exercise in the occult, the rent officer would ignore the personal circumstances of the tenant but have regard to the age, size, character, locality, and state of repair of the dwelling. They were required to set a rent which would be fair to both landlord and tenant as if supply and demand roughly balanced; in fact, a market rent in the absence of scarcity.

In the early days, most of the applications came from tenants and the rent officers happily set about reducing large numbers of high rents which had resulted from the 1957 Act.

However, dissatisfied landlords or tenants could appeal to Rent Assessment Committees (RACs) appointed by the civil servants. Sir Sydney Littlewood, a well-known valuer, chaired the London Rent Assessment Committee (by far the most important), which set the tone for the other RACs. The London RAC increased many of the rents fixed by rent officers. Thereafter, it was mainly landlords, not tenants who went to the rent officer asking them to set a 'fair' rent for their properties.

Not for the first time, the civil service had defeated the intentions of a Minister. Crossman was unhappy but went on claiming that his fair rent idea was basically sound. However, the disquiet was enough for the Labour government to set up another committee, the Francis Committee in 1969, to consider how the Rent Act 1965 was working. By the time it reported, two years later, a Conservative government was in power. The report concluded that although a lot of rent officers found themselves unable to quantify scarcity and therefore made no allowance for it, all was well – though allowing for the effect of scarcity had been the very basis of the Crossman formula. The report was accepted with alacrity.

The Conservative government went on to pass the Housing Finance Act 1972. This extended the fair rent concept to council housing (see chapter two) and it also made provision for a phased transfer of the remaining old controlled tenancies into the fair rent system called the 'regulated tenancy system'.

This phased transfer was halted temporarily by Labour when it returned to power in 1974, to give itself time to make a full review of the working of the Rent Acts but it was all change once more, as a Conservative government took over in 1979.

Effects of the Housing Act 1980

By 1980, there were 400,000 houses with rents still controlled under the old system. The Conservatives' 1980 Act converted them, at a stroke, to regulated tenancies for which fair rents would be set whatever the condition of the properties. Landlords would also be allowed to apply for re-registration (for a higher rent) after two years instead of three. It was the end of the original rent control system which had started in 1915 as a temporary measure.

Two new types of tenancy were also introduced. One was the protected shorthold tenancy which allowed the landlord to let a vacant property at a fair rent for a fixed term of one to five years and regain possession at the end. It was expected that this would make shortholds an attractive proposition for landlords but it was not particularly successful. They still preferred to sell rather than re-let since they were not happy with fair rents even though these were likely to be three times as much as the previous controlled rents. After a couple of years, further legislation provided that, outside London, a landlord need not apply for a fair rent as a condition of letting on shorthold terms.

The other innovation was the assured tenancy. The fair rent system would not apply and rents would be freely negotiated between landlord and tenant. The landlord could let for any period and, at the end of the period, the tenant would have a right to a new tenancy on terms to be agreed; or if not agreed, on terms to be settled by the County Court with any rent fixed by the Court set at market level.

At first the assured tenancy applied only to new dwellings. In 1986, it was extended to existing dwellings if they had been improved or modernised by the landlord but it was available only to landlords approved by the Secretary of State.

It was claimed that these two new forms of tenancy would at last slow down, and perhaps even reverse, the decline of the private rented sector. But the downward trend continued, as table 6 shows:

Figure 6 Private Renting in Great Britain

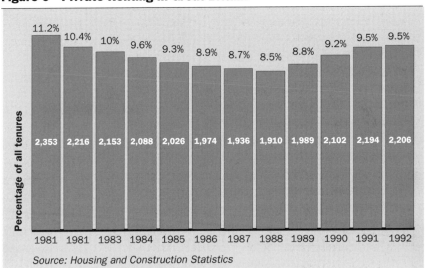

Source: Housing and Construction Statistics

The Housing Act 1988

In 1987 the government issued a White Paper setting out its intentions for what was to become the Housing Act 1988. It covered all tenures.

On the private rented sector, the government proposed to deregulate private lettings while protecting existing tenants. It planned to put new life into what it now calls the 'independent rented sector', housing owned by private landlords and housing associations. Public sector housing would be dispersed to other landlords and the purchase and management of property by the private sector and housing associations would broaden the choice available to tenants.

While protecting the position of existing tenants, the government proposed to make progress towards market rents by building on the two concepts of assured and shorthold tenancies.

The changes made in pursuance of these objectives are set out in the Housing Act 1988 which came into effect on 15 January 1989.

For new lettings, the main change is that the regulated tenancy (subject to fair rents) no longer applies. Landlords can choose either:

- an assured tenancy, with rents freely negotiated but with security of tenure protected. At the end of a tenancy, the tenant would be entitled to a further assured tenancy. A spouse would have an automatic right to succeed to the tenancy on the death of the assured tenant. There is no right to a second succession; and other relatives have no right at all to succeed.

- an assured shorthold tenancy for which the minimum period for letting has been reduced from one year to six months. There will not be a fair rent though either party will have the right at any time to get the rent fixed at a 'market level which takes account of the limited security of tenure which the tenant has been offered'. Such a rent will be set by the Rent Assessment Committee.

Landlords offering assured tenancies no longer have to be approved by the Secretary of State and the basic fitness standard has been abolished. Most of the remaining controls over new lettings by resident landlords (where the landlord lives in part of a dwelling and lets other parts) have been removed.

For tenancies which were in existence before 15 January 1989 the main changes are:

- the fair rent system still applies, but when a tenancy ends, the landlord can re-let on either an assured or assured shorthold basis.

- the spouse will continue as the 'protected' tenant, the new description for what was the 'regulated' tenant, when the tenant dies. Other relatives will have a right to succeed but only if they have lived there for the last two years and only as assured tenants. Second successions are only possible where the person was a member of both the original tenant's family and the first successor's family.

- for existing shorthold tenants there is no security of tenure beyond the brief period of the tenancy.

There are also provisions to protect tenants from harassment by landlords who seek to obtain possession or re-let at higher rents. And landlords are entitled to charge 'key money' for the granting of assured or shorthold tenancy.

Housing benefit for private tenants

Housing benefit is paid by local councils to help private tenants on low incomes with their rents. Council tenants are also entitled to help. This system is described more fully in the next chapter.

Rents rose steeply as 'fair rents' replaced the old controlled rents and did so again after the 1989 deregulation. This was entirely intentional since the government's declared aim was to raise rents high enough to reverse the decline of private renting.

Higher rents would obviously require higher housing benefit if serious hardship to tenants was to be avoided. The cost to the taxpayer has been substantial. There have been repeated assurances that housing benefit will continue to provide an adequate 'safety net', and the 1987 White Paper (para. 3.18) said that 'the housing benefit system will continue to provide help to those who need it'. But it also said that landlords should not be able to increase the rents of benefit recipients to unreasonable levels at the expense of the taxpayer.

The Housing Act 1988 requires rent officers to scrutinise the levels of rent which are being supported by housing benefit. When a rent is excessive, the local authority only gets subsidy on the appropriate market rent. The council, therefore, has to pay benefit based on the rent officer's concept of a market rent, not the landlord's. Not only do the rent officers decide what the market rent should be, they are also required to consider whether the dwelling is too large for the tenant's 'reasonable' needs.

This is a sorry business. For low income tenants, assured rents have come to mean an assurance of more hardship, uncertainty and insecurity.

'Perks' for the private landlord

As long ago as 1985, the Greater London Council, just before its demise, did a survey which revealed that the majority of new lets in the London area were evading the Rents Act altogether by devices such as letting on licence, holiday lettings or simply ignoring the law altogether and operating on a market rent basis. Nothing happened to them and the 1988 Act gave landlords the green light to raise rents.

A further perk for landlords came with the introduction of the poll tax in April 1990 (1989 in Scotland). They were mostly charging inclusive rents (i.e rent plus rates) and handing over the rates element to the local authority. With the arrival of the poll tax, liability fell on each individual and landlords no longer had to hand over part of the inclusive rent. Enterprising landlords simply went on charging as much as before thus giving themselves a handsome rent increase. The government's only response to this scandalous business was an expression of pious hope that landlords would behave reasonably.

Has government policy worked?

The aim of the government's policy was to stem, and if possible reverse, the decline in the private rented sector by allowing the charging of market rents for new lettings. Private landlords want, like other investors, not merely an adequate return on the amount originally invested but a return on the current value of their property.

Unfortunately, the government seems to be unaware that its policy is hopelessly flawed since, in seeking to meet the landlord's requirements, it depends on rent levels which most people, who need to rent, cannot pay. There is, dimly, a realisation that in present conditions the adequate 'safety net' which housing benefit should provide was never intended to cope with a situation produced by free markets. Hence the new role for rent officers, referred to above, which inevitably prevents market forces from operating freely.

There is also no apparent understanding that the tax privileges which subsidise home-ownership are not available to private landlords. It costs less to buy than to pay free market rents. Consider the elementary arithmetic.

Let us assume that a purchaser buys a house for £40,000. Mortgage interest is, at the time of writing, about 7.5 per cent. The approximate annual outgoings with a 95 per cent mortgage for 25 years are shown in the table below.

A private landlord providing the same size and quality of house would have little chance of financing the operation so favourably, but assume 7.5 per cent for this comparison.

Table 7 Home-ownership Versus Private Renting

Annual costs	Home-owner	Landlord
Mortgage repayment after tax relief on interest	2,993	—
Loan charges – no tax relief	—	3,451
Repairs & maintenance, say	500	500
Management, say	—	500
Total	3493	4451

For the home-owner, in this simple example, the weekly cost turns out to be £67.17 whereas the landlord's costs are £85.60. There is scope for argument about the precise sums involved, but it is clear that in order to make a reasonable profit landlords need to charge rents that are not competitive with house purchase. The rent, clearly, would have to be well over £85. Who is going to pay such a rent for a house that will never be theirs when £67 a week will buy it?

In London and the South-East, the mortgage repayment figures would be considerably higher. There, the advantage in house purchase would be rather less, proportionately, because the £30,000 mortgage ceiling for tax relief would still apply on the much larger mortgage. But the advantage in buying would still be considerable; the landlord would need a rent which would be far beyond the reach of householders who need to rent.

Subsidies for some landlords?

Perhaps the government does, after all, recognise that subsidy for owner-occupation but not for private renting is one of the basic problems. In 1988 the then Chancellor, Nigel Lawson, extended the Business Expansion Scheme (BES) to rented housing. The scheme had been introduced to encourage the formation of small companies but the rules were changed to allow the BES to apply to the provision of rented housing with a ceiling of investment of £5 million instead of the £500,000 which applied to other small businesses. There were limits on the prices of dwellings which could be bought under the scheme – £125,000 in London, £85,000 outside.

Tax relief was given at the marginal rate on investment by an individual in any year of up to £40,000. To increase the incentive in the first few months, the higher marginal rate, 60 per cent, applied if the investment was made by 26 October 1988. Subsequently it was 40 per cent.

The practical effect was that with 40 per cent tax relief, for example, the investor putting £40,000 into a scheme got a reduction in their tax bill of £16,000; so the investment cost only £24,000. To put it another way, for £24,000 invested there was an added capital subsidy of £16,000.

As a further attraction, and to discourage early disinvestment, there was exemption from capital gains tax if the investor left the investment with the BES company for at least five years. The prospect of capital gains was, of course, a very important consideration.

The scheme certainly brought additional private resources into the rented market and the Minister of Housing claimed in 1994 that some 40,000 new dwellings had been provided under the scheme. But the new landlords – often estate agents, solicitors and valuers – are unlikely to provide accommodation at 'affordable rents' for those with low incomes. Early evidence on how the BES was working showed that rents in London were just over £100 per week. Some of the money raised under BES has been on behalf of universities and housing associations (unintended beneficiaries of the subsidy) but more commercial investors were quite frank about their intention to cater for the upwardly mobile who could afford market rents and could be expected to move on after a couple of years.

The BES was wound up in November 1993 and housing was explicitly excluded from the government's replacement initiative. Nevertheless, the government does seem to have scored a 'first', breaking new ground by subsidising private landlords who provide rented accommodation for tenants who clearly could afford to be home-owners, but not for tenants who could not afford home-ownership. How much of the new housing generated by BES will continue to be available for renting in the longer run remains to be seen but the way the scheme was set up suggests that most will be sold off for owner occupation as investors seek to cash in their shares.

5 Housing Benefit

Today, most people who rent their homes rely on housing benefit, to help them meet their housing costs. Housing benefit is a means tested benefit, aimed at those with the lowest incomes, which is rapidly withdrawn as income rises. This chapter aims to give only an outline of the housing benefit system in Britain. A detailed guide would require far more space than is available here and, in any case, there are specialist publications which do the job very well (for example, *Guide to Housing Benefit and Council Tax Benefit 1994-95* by John Zebedee and Martin Ward, Institute of Housing/SHAC, £10.95).

Means tested assistance has only been available to tenants in all tenures since 1972 and housing benefit itself has existed only since 1982. The introduction of housing benefit followed years of debate but, in the event, the scheme that was adopted had many shortcomings and it was implemented in so short a time-scale that there was considerable administrative confusion. Less than a year after the full scheme started, a review was set up, and important changes were made to housing benefit as part of a wider reform of social security.

The Social Security Act 1986 led to the introduction of the reformed housing benefit system in April 1988. Further changes took effect from April 1990 (1989 in Scotland), when rate rebates were replaced by community charge (poll tax) benefit (which was not strictly part of housing benefit, since the poll tax was not a tax on property). With abolition of the poll tax from 1 April 1993 the community charge (poll tax) benefit was replaced by council tax benefit. The introduction of the council tax meant the restoration of a tax linked to property values after the disastrous excursion into the poll tax which was levied on all individuals.

Background

Housing is expensive and the origins of housing benefit lie in debates in the early part of this century about how best to help low income households to afford decent accommodation. The introduction of housing subsidies in 1919 meant that the rents of council houses were generally lower than they would otherwise have been but, at first, there was no attempt to ensure that subsidies helped the least well off. Indeed, in the 1920s, the costs of building new houses were so high that even subsidised rents were generally beyond the reach of the poor. Council housing thus began as subsidised housing for the better off skilled workers.

However, in 1930 the Labour government passed a Housing Act requiring councils to launch slum clearance programmes. Rehousing families from the slums inevitably meant that councils became landlords to growing numbers of poorer people. The government therefore gave way to demands to provide rent rebates for those who could least afford the rent of a new council house.

Councils could grant rent rebates on whatever terms they chose; there was no compulsion to provide rebates nor any clear guidance on the form that rebate schemes might take. And there was no central government subsidy to pay for rebates; if an authority chose to grant rent rebates to certain tenants then it did so either by redistributing existing general Exchequer subsidy or by increasing the amount contributed from the rates in support of housing. Central government was not, at that time, strongly committed to means tested rent assistance. The 1930 Act set a pattern which endured for forty years, until the introduction of a mandatory rent rebate scheme, with its own specific subsidy in 1972.

During the 1930s, both councils and their tenants were opposed to rent rebate schemes and for a while, after the second world war, interest in providing rebates declined still further. It was in the mid-1950s that a Conservative government revived debate about the best way to provide help with housing costs. The Conservative Party has always regarded the universal provision of public services, like health care and education, as wasteful. It emphasised the targeting of public resources on those in greatest need and, in the mid-1950s, it urged councils to extend the availability of rent rebate schemes while raising rents generally. There was an important policy shift away from general subsidy and towards means tested benefits.

However, if help with housing costs was to be means tested, should the local authorities be responsible for providing such help? In the 1950s and 1960s, there was a protracted disagreement between local authorities and the

National Assistance Board (replaced by the Supplementary Benefits Commission in 1966). The local authority view was that rebates were a social security benefit and should be provided by the appropriate authority. The NAB argued that councils had a responsibility to distribute housing subsidies to those in need of such help. This long-running dispute illustrates the ambiguity of rent rebates, occupying as they do the ground where housing and social security meet. It also highlights the development of two quite separate, but overlapping systems, of providing help with housing costs.

The need to resolve this problem intensified after 1972. Local authorities had to provide rent rebates for their own tenants and give rent allowances for private tenants. Before this, there had been no help for private tenants who were working or who, for other reasons, did not qualify for supplementary benefit. Many more tenants now became eligible for benefit.

The parallel existence of the local authority and social security systems also gave rise to what became known as the 'better off' problem. Councils gave rent rebates and rent allowances on a means test which took into account gross income while supplementary benefit operated on a measure of net income. Also, the rebate/allowance scheme was more generous than supplementary benefit to people on rather higher incomes. This was a recipe for confusion. Although many people qualified for both benefits, they could only receive one and they had to choose whether to claim a rebate/allowance or supplementary benefit but it was often difficult to tell which would make them better off. It was even difficult for skilled housing advisers to decide which benefit people should claim.

The 'better off problem' resulted in hundreds of thousands of people receiving the 'wrong' benefit, and this became one of the main reasons for reform which could produce a unified housing benefit. In the late 1970s, the Supplementary Benefits Commission argued for a unified benefit to be administered by the local housing authorities. As well as producing a simpler and fairer system, the SBC wanted it to provide help for low income home-owners who were generally ignored by the existing systems. Home-owners could claim rate rebates, and the few who were entitled to supplementary benefit could be helped with mortgage interest but most low income home-owners were very unfairly treated by the system of mortgage interest tax relief which was so generous to higher earners.

When the Conservative government produced its proposals (*Assistance with Housing Costs*, 1981) they were largely confined to administrative reform in all sectors. The opportunity for fundamental reform of housing finance was spurned in favour of a limited reorganisation of responsibilities for the administration of housing benefits plus a certain amount of redistribution towards the poorest at the expense of the slightly better off.

The housing benefit scheme was introduced in two stages, in November 1982 and April 1983, following the Social Security and Housing Benefits Act 1982. *The Times* described it as 'the biggest administrative fiasco in the history of the welfare state.' (20 January 1984) The complexity of the new system and the speed with which it was introduced, among other things, contributed to this 'fiasco'. Councils were simply not given enough time, nor enough help, to allow them to implement the system successfully. The government then made a series of cuts in the benefit levels which made it even more difficult for councils and claimants alike.

The new scheme retained the two separate means tests that were inherited from the old system. After 1982 there were two categories of housing benefit claimant, known as 'standard' and 'certificated' cases. Standard housing benefit was effectively the old rent rebate (or allowance) and rates rebate, while certificated housing benefit was like the housing part of supplementary benefit. These two separate forms of housing benefit, based on different means tests, meant that people with similar incomes could be treated quite differ-

ently depending on whether they were entitled to supplementary benefit or not.

The current housing benefit scheme

A review of the 1982 scheme was completed in 1985 and proposals were incorporated into the Social Security Act 1986. This Act also reformed other parts of the social security system including the replacement of supplementary benefit by income support and the introduction of the social fund; family credit replaced family income supplement.

The new housing benefit scheme was designed to be simpler to administer and understand; to treat people in similar circumstances in the same way whether or not they were working; to direct help to where it was most needed; to improve accountancy; and to encourage efficient administration.

The new scheme is better than the pre-1988 system as there is no longer a distinction between standard and certificated cases. All claimants are now assessed on the basis of the income support means test. Where a claimant's income is equivalent to, or less than, what is known as the 'applicable amount', then housing benefit provides 100 per cent of eligible housing costs (i.e. in most cases HB covers the full rent).

As income rises above the applicable amount, the level of benefit is reduced. In the jargon of social security, benefit is said to 'taper'. In the case of housing benefit, it tapers at a rate of 65p for every £1 of extra income. So, if a person was entitled to housing benefit of £10 per week, they would lose all entitlement when their income reached an extra £16 a week. (16 x 0.65 = £10.40).

For council tax benefit (CTB) the rate of taper is 20 per cent. So, a person claiming both HB and CTB would find that their benefit was reduced by 85p for every extra £1 of income. To understand how the scheme works it is useful to look at who can claim HB, how the scheme is administered, how claims are calculated and how benefit is paid.

The housing benefit scheme applies to both public and private sector tenants. This covers a wide range of landlords, including councils, housing associations, new towns, commercial landlords, co-ops and hostels. Home-owners who previously got HB for rates can now only claim the separate council tax benefit.

There are two routes to claiming housing benefit. People claiming income support normally claim HB (and CTB) at the same time from the Department of Social Security (DSS). But housing benefit is not administered by the DSS so forms have to be passed on to the local authorities which are the responsible agencies. The second route to claiming is, therefore, to make a direct approach to the local authority. People not claiming income support usually do this.

Councils must take several things into account when assessing a claim. Claimants on income support are easiest to assess because details such as income and capital assets will have been verified by the DSS when they assess the income support claim before the papers are passed to the local council. However, the council still has to investigate the person's rent and council tax and details of any non-dependent adults living in the same house. People on income support get maximum benefit which covers eligible rent, minus any deduction for non-dependants, and 100 per cent of council tax. People not on income support might have to pay significant amounts towards both rent and coucil tax, depending on their circumstances. However, single people living alone and households with only one adult are entitled to a 25 per cent reduction on their council tax, irrespective of income. The council tax is more generous than the poll tax, to the extent that CTB provides up to 100 per cent assistance, whereas under the poll tax the maximum level of rebate was 80 per cent. On the other hand, the taper applied to CTB is 20 per cent whereas the poll tax benefit taper was 15 per cent.

To calculate entitlement, the council has to determine:
- income
- capital
- the 'applicable amount'
- eligible costs
- details of any non-dependants.

Income is calculated on weekly income from all sources such as wages, benefits, pensions, and assumed (not actual) interest on savings above £3,000. Some forms of income are disregarded (a small earnings disregard applies where claimants are in employment; the amount depends upon the type of household and is not proportional to the level of earnings). The term capital applies to savings, property, shares and any lump sum payments from redundancy or retirement. Anyone with more than £16,000 of capital cannot get either HB or CTB but some capital is disregarded, most notably the claimant's home. It is interesting to note that while benefit rates and applicable amounts are regularly uprated, the savings figures have remained unchanged since the previous edition of this guide in 1990 despite the effect of inflation.

The 'applicable amount' is the official measure of the amount that people in different circumstances need in order to meet basic living requirements. The applicable amount for any particular claimant is a combination of the relevant personal allowance plus any relevant premiums. In 1994-95, the personal allowance for a single person over the age of 25 is £45.70, and for a couple where at least one partner is over 18, £71.50. There are different dependants' allowances for each child in a family. The premiums are extra amounts in recognition of higher costs for certain claimants and households. So, there are premiums for lone parents, disabled children, disabled adults and pensioners.

Eligible costs cover rent and council tax. Since the deregulation of private sector rents at the start of 1989, rent officers have stopped fixing fair rents for new lettings and have the job of determining market rents for HB purposes (see also chapter three). In cases where the claimant's accommodation is too large, or where the rent is unreasonably high compared with rents for suitable alternative accommodation, the council is not obliged to pay HB on the full rent. The eligible rent then would be set by the rent officer rather than the market.

Table 8   Housing Benefit Calculation

	£	£
Assessed net income	85.00	
(£90 less earnings disregard of £5.00)		
Applicable amount	45.70	
Excess income		
£85.00 less £45.70	39.30	
Housing benefit –		
100% of weekly eligible rent		50.00
less – non-dependant deduction 13.00		
less – 65% of excess income 25.55		
		38.55
Housing benefit entitlement		11.45

The woman is entitled to £5 earnings disregard as a single claimant and her applicable amount of £45.70 is the amount for single claimants over 25. Her son is deemed to be contributing £13 because he earns between £108 and £138.99 per week.

The final item to be considered is any non-dependants living in the claimant's household. Certain categories of non-dependants are assumed to be making a contribution to the rent and reductions are made in the claimant's HB entitlement depending on the circumstances of the non-dependant.

Table 8 provides an example of a housing benefit calculation based on a woman and her adult son aged 20 living together. Their rent is £50 per week. The mother's take home pay is £90 and the son's gross pay is £110. They have savings of under £3,000, and so there is no notional income from interest.

Turning to a sample council tax benefit calculation, let us consider a family of four people, a couple and their children aged 4 and 20. The mother is not in employment and her only income is £10.20 child benefit. The father's net pay is £130.00 per week and the eldest child earns £100 gross. The council tax is £650 per annum.

Table 9   Council Tax Benefit Calculation

	£	£	£
Assessed net income			
Earnings		130.00	
Child benefit		10.20	
		140.20	
less earnings disregard		10.00	
Total		130.20	
Applicable amount			
couple	71.70		
child under 11	15.65		
family premium	10.05	97.40	
Excess income		32.80	
Council tax benefit			
Weekly council tax			12.47
less non-dependant deduction 1.15			
less 20% of excess income	6.56		7.71
Weekly council tax benefit			4.76
Annual council tax benefit			247.52

These are just illustrative, and very straightforward, examples, and different circumstances will give different results. Readers requiring more detailed information should consult the specialist guide referred to at the beginning of this chapter.

Paying for housing benefit

Until 1972, local authorities were not given any specific financial support for paying rebates to poorer tenants and had to use general housing subsidy to fund rebates. From 1972 onwards there was a specific rent rebate subsidy but it was not until the introduction of HB in 1982 that the government moved rent rebate subsidy into the social security budget within the national public expenditure accounts. This made good sense because it left the DoE responsible for housing subsidy and the DHSS (later the DSS) took on responsibility for what was properly recognised as a social security benefit. It would have been logical to take the next step and to transfer administrative responsibility for HB to the DSS as well.

However, in the Local Government and Housing Act 1989, the government took several paces backwards by merging rent rebate subsidy with housing subsidy in the new housing revenue account subsidy (HRAS). HRAS consists of two elements, the housing element and the rent rebate element (see chapter 2). The rebate element is always a positive amount but the housing element can be negative and, in some cases, can exceed the rebate element. What the council actually receives depends upon the sum of these two numbers so although the total entitlement of all tenants may be very substantial, it is possible for the authority to receive no subsidy at all.

Critics of the government's position have argued that the better off tenants will thus find themselves paying the rebates of their poorer neighbours. It has also been argued that this move reflects Treasury determination to get its hands on any HRA surpluses rather than allowing councils to use them to improve local services. The government's argument for creaming off HRA surpluses was that it was necessary in order to avoid providing a cushion for inefficiency. Needless to say that this system does not apply in the private rented sector where the deregulation of rents was designed specifically to allow landlords to make profits. It is curious that surpluses can be a cushion for inefficiency in one tenure and yet be a necessary stimulus to investment in another.

There is another flaw in the current system as it applies to the private sector. The government's aim was to establish a deregulated private rented market but there is a conflict between a free market and a benefit system which provides 100 per cent assistance to the poorest tenants. If some tenants are guaranteed all their housing costs, then there is no market based restraint on rents which is why the government has had to divert the rent officer service into the task of fixing maximum rents for benefit purposes.

The obvious way forward in this situation would be to reimpose a system based on regulated rents in the private sector but that, of course, would require a change of government. The housing benefit system has become the target of Treasury attempts to cut back on welfare spending. The Treasury is very concerned not just about the rapidly rising aggregate cost of housing benefit but also the way that spending on housing benefit is demand-led, i.e. it depends on the number of eligible claimants. The Treasury dislikes open-ended spending commitments.

The rapidly rising cost of housing benefit has propelled it to the forefront of government thinking. Housing benefit expenditure was £8.8 billion in 1993/94, accounting for 10 per cent of all social security spending. Not only has the spending on housing benefit doubled since 1989/90 but it is now about twice the level of mortgage interest relief.

The problem is that the government wants to have it both ways – it wants higher rents to encourage a revival of private renting but it also wants to avoid the inevitable rise in housing benefit expenditure that follows from those same higher rents.

6 Owner-occupation

By 1992, owner-occupation in Great Britain accounted for 15,441 million dwellings, just over 66 per cent of the housing stock, reflecting its history as the fastest growing and most popular sector. This is not surprising, for not only does it offer the householder more freedom and choice than any other tenure, it has also long been the most profitable investment that ordinary people ever make.

The extent of the expansion has been spectacular:

Figure 10   Increase in Owner-occupation in Great Britain

Total stock of dwellings in Great Britain

Owner-occupied sector

Source: Housing and Construction Statistics, Sept. Qtr 1988, Part 2 (Table 2)

Year	Total stock of dwellings	Owner-occupied sector	%
1914	8,500	3,300	25.6%
1944	12,900	3,300	25.6%
1951	13,900	4,100	29.5%
1961	16,400	7,000	42.7%
1971	18,999	9,598	50.5%
1981	21,184	11,935	56.4%
1988	22,518	15,105	64.8%
1990	22,928	15,105	65.9%
1992	23,301	15,441	66.3%

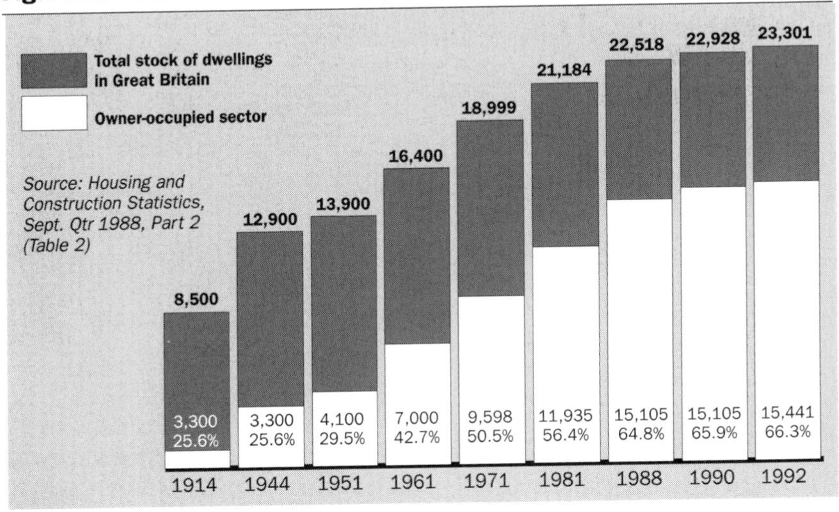

The provision of housing requires massive finance. Virtually all houses are bought with borrowed money and, until recent years, nearly all of this came from building societies. Local authorities, insurance companies and banks made a relatively small contribution. However, there have been enormous

83

changes since the early 1980s with the banks especially making a dramatic increase in their share of the market.

Although the building societies' share of the business has declined recently to between 50 and 60 per cent, it is still by far the largest; and it has been the societies which developed the procedures which the market follows. We start by looking at the way they operate.

Growth of the building societies

Building societies started in a small way in the late 18th century with small groups of working people joining together, each member paying a weekly subscription. When there was enough money to buy or build a house, one of the members would take it over. Each would continue to contribute until all had been housed and the group would then disband. These early societies were called 'terminating' societies, and out of their success developed the 'permanent' societies, raising funds by offering a savings bank facility. But progress was still very slow until after the end of the first world war when their expansion really started. Yet this was as nothing to what followed the second world war or even the more explosive growth of the last 20 years (see Table 11).

Table 11   Building Societies' Progress

	Advances during year £m	Total assets at year end £m
1900	9	60
1920	25	87
1940	21	756
1960	560	3,166
1980	9,614	53,793
1988	49,376	188,844
1992	34,989	262,515

Figures after 1988 exclude Abbey National PLC.
Source: Housing Finance, May 1994 (Council of Mortgage lenders)

In earlier years there were some colourful characters in the industry – not a bit like it is today – and there were some spectacular (and sometimes hilarious) episodes involving fraud. But the dramatic success of the last 30 years has been solidly built on a first rate service to savers and a reputation for reliability. Although building societies have grown rapidly in terms of the volume of lending for house purchase, there are now fewer societies than there were a century ago. In 1900 there were about 2,000 societies and by 1992 there were just 105. It is also important to remember that building society business is dominated by a small number of very large societies.

The way lenders work

At first sight, the whole basis on which building societies have operated, accepting money which is mostly repayable on demand or at very short notice and lending it for long periods, is the very opposite of what is normally regarded as sound practice. It is borrowing short to lend long. But there is a safeguard which transforms the situation. Each loan is secured by a mortgage. It gives a 'legal charge' to the lender on the property by which, if the borrower fails to comply with the terms of the mortgage, the lender can take over the property, sell it, and clear the debt from the proceeds of the sale. In this procedure the society is said to foreclose on the loan and to take the house into possession (not 'repossession', a term incorrectly used by the media.)

Traditional building society mortgages contain a 'variable interest clause', and it is this which allows the lenders to make loans for 25 years or even more, although the greatest part of their funds come from investors who are entitled to repayment immediately or at very short notice. When interest rates rise, the lending institution can avoid withdrawals by investors by promptly increasing its own interest rates to investors. It can do this quite safely because it can at the same time give notice to all its borrowers, under the variable interest clause in their mortgages, that the interest they pay will also go up. But in periods of frequent changes in interest rates the societies found that it was expensive to notify every borrower every time the rate changed. An increasing proportion of borrowers now find that their repayment changes only once a year – irrespective of movements in interest rates – the effect of past changes is taken into account when fixing the repayment for the coming year.

However, a recent trend has seen the rising popularity of mortgages with interest rates fixed for periods up to five years. Clearly borrowers are keener to agree fixed interest rates when rates are seen to be low, as they have been in the last year or so, and the availability of fixed rate mortgages has increased because of changes in the way that societies raise their funds.

In the past building societies raised nearly all their funds from individual investors (often from people saving the deposit to buy their first home). Since the deregulation of financial services in the 1980s, things have become much more complicated and now mortgage lenders raise much more of their funds from the money markets.

Deregulation also led to the breakdown of the system of agreed interest rates. The building societies until 1983 published recommended rates of interest to give a measure of stability in a vast financial market which affects millions of people. The members of the Building Societies Association followed the recommendation fairly closely but since 1983 each lender began fixing its own rates according to market conditions.

Until the early 1980s, most borrowers had repayment mortgages which meant that the loan was paid off gradually over a period. A borrower with a repayment mortgage pays the same amount each month throughout the life of the loan (assuming that interest rates do not change). Each payment consists of two parts: a repayment element and an amount of interest on the loan still outstanding. In the first year, payments contain a high level of interest and only a very small amount towards repayment of the principal. But as the years go by, the interest element decreases while the principal element becomes the dominating proportion of the repayment. The whole calculation ensures that by the end of the period the loan will have been paid off.

There is another method, which became increasingly popular in the 1980s, called the low cost endowment mortgage. Instead of repaying the principal a little at a time, the borrower takes out a life assurance policy which, besides giving life cover during the loan period, will at the end of the term yield a sum which will pay off the loan. So the method means paying interest on the whole amount of the loan throughout the loan period and an annual premium on the assurance policy. The term low cost endowment means that the borrower reduces the cost of premiums on the life assurance policy by taking out what is known as a with profits endowment policy for a sum assured that is less than would be required to repay the loan in full – the profits element (a sort of annual bonus) is expected to more than cover the difference. But there is no guarantee and there have been growing concerns about the capacity of some low cost endowment schemes to generate enough money to enable borrowers to meet their debts.

Tax relief on the mortgage interest will be much greater with an endowment mortgage because interest will not decrease year by year. By 1981, about a quarter of borrowers were choosing the endowment mortgage; by 1989 it was about 80 per cent but by 1993 the proportion had fallen back to 54 per cent.

One of the largest building societies gives the following examples of the relative costs of repayment mortgages and low cost endowment mortgages (see table 12)

Table 12 Typical Mortgage Costs

	Repayment Mortgage	Low Cost Endowment
Mortgage		
Amount of Loan	£38,000	£38,000
Current interest rate (variable)	7.64%	7.64%
Monthly payments		
Principal and net interest	£249.39	—
Net interest	—	£203.74
Life assurance premium	—	59.55
Optional mortgage protection premium	13.92	—
Total monthly cost	£263.31	£263.29

Figures based on 95 per cent loan on a £40,000 house bought by a couple aged 30.

The building society providing the above figures also calculated that the total cost of the purchase over 25 years would exceed £87,000.

The figures show monthly repayments net of mortgage interest relief at the rate of 20 per cent on the first £30,000 of the loan. Beyond the £30,000 ceiling no relief is available (this is discussed later in this chapter).

The lending on endowment mortgages is done by the building society, bank or other lender, with the life assurance cover provided by an insurance company. There have been criticisms that the rapid expansion of the method is not wholly unconnected with the fact that lenders, estate agents and solicitors earn a substantial commission from the insurance company on policies sold.

The borrowers

Most would-be home-owners, having found a suitable house, approach a lender for a loan. Lenders used to be prepared to lend 75 per cent, perhaps 80 per cent, of the value of the property. Borrowers would have to find the rest themselves as well as other costs like solicitors' and valuers' fees.

The lender wanted to ensure that the borrower would be able to meet the cost of repayments. For many years a loan of 2.25–2.5 times the borrower's annual income was provided. If there were two incomes involved, usually the second income, or part of it, could be taken into account. Earnings of say £8,000 a year would have been good for a loan of £18,000 to £20,000 if the value of the property justified it.

That was the position until about 1984 but the house price explosion has made for great changes. It has meant vastly increased demand in terms of finance not only from the first-time buyers but also from owners who see an advantage in 'trading up' to larger or better quality dwellings. Incomes have been rising too. And building societies and other lenders, observing the unprecedented rise in house prices and, consequently, the value of their security – the dwelling – felt safe in lending three times the annual income. And this was three times a larger income than it would have been two or three years earlier.

Former owner-occupiers usually have higher incomes than first-time buyers. They are now able to put down £27,000 on average towards the cost of a house, from the proceeds of the sale of the former house, as compared with about £9,000 in the case of first-time buyers.

Subsidies for owner-occupiers

Until relatively recently it was widely believed that home-owners were not recipients of any help from the public purse. Now, however, the position has changed and few people, including the government, deny that the tax system provides massive subsidy. During the 1980s Mrs Thatcher resisted growing demands from housing analysts and the Treasury for reform of mortgage interest tax relief. As recently as the 1992 general election the Conservative manifesto pledged the party to a continuing commitment to mortgage interest relief. The political importance of the votes of home-owners made it difficult for any party to campaign for the reform of the mortgage interest relief system.

Table 13   Building Society Loan Advances

	No. of advances	Average income of buyer	Average dwelling price	Average advance	Advance as % of dwelling	Advance times income
	000s	£	£	£	%	
First time buyers						
1977	355	4,800	10,857	8,515	78.4	1.8
1986	619	11,669	27,444	23,640	86.1	2.0
1987	505	12,444	30,097	25,485	84.8	2.0
1988	580	13,990	35,807	30,374	84.8	2.2
1993	305	17,981	47,597	38,801	81.5	2.16
Former owner-occupiers						
1977	382	5,558	16,246	9,101	46.0	1.6
1986	612	4,165	45,200	27,146	60.2	1.9
1987	542	15,004	49,987	29,487	59.0	2.0
1988	650	17,108	61,540	36,013	58.5	2.1
1993	259	24,492	77,284	50,124	64.9	2.05

Source: Housing Finance July 1989 (Council of Mortgage Lenders)
1993 figures – Source: Housing Finance, May 1994

Schedule A tax

The ownership of property always used to be taxed on its rental value. The tax was called Schedule A tax, as distinct from Schedule D which is levied on profits or Schedule E on earnings.

Owner-occupiers do not pay rent. Of two people in identical houses, worth a rent of say £2,000 a year, one owning and one renting, the owner will nominally have £2,000 a year more to spend than the one who is a tenant (discounting mortgage repayments and maintenance costs). It has been argued that the owner has sacrificed income by putting money into buying a house instead of investing it in some other way. That is perfectly true. But if the money had been invested so that it produced £2,000 annual income there would have been tax to pay on that income; whereas no tax is payable on the no less real increase in disposable income which results from owning instead of renting.

In 1955, a Royal Commission on the Taxation of Profits and Income recommended that taxation of the benefit of ownership (on what it called the 'imputed rental') was right and should continue as an essential element of a fair taxation system.

Nevertheless, in 1962, Chancellor announced the abolition of Schedule A income tax on owner-occupied houses. Since then, the owner has enjoyed a tax-free increase in net disposable income as compared with what happens to a tenant. They are being given favourable treatment as compared with other householders who have to pay rent. It is important to remember here that tax breaks given to particular groups mean that tax payers generally have to pay more to make good what is lost.

Tax relief on mortgage interest

A householder, while the legal owner, might not own outright, if the property is still on mortgage – nearly half of all home-owners are still paying off their mortgages. There is ownership in a legal sense but, in practical terms, the householder is only in the process of becoming the owner, not yet enjoying the full benefits of ownership. It would clearly not be equitable to tax mortgagors as if they did own outright. They are saving themselves a rent but they have to meet repayments on a mortgage.

Before the abolition of Schedule A tax this was not a problem. In accordance with normal taxation practice, though mortgagors were taxable under Schedule A as owners, they were entitled to a reduction of the assessment in respect of the interest being paid on the mortgage loan. In the parlance of the tax people, they were entitled to set off the expense incurred in acquiring an asset against any tax levied on income arising from ownership of that asset.

So when Parliament abolished Schedule A tax, there remained no logical reason for giving tax relief on mortgage interest except as an inducement to people to buy houses on mortgage. There is nothing wrong in principle with assisting home-ownership. What has been wrong, and dishonest, is the constant stressing of the heavy cost of subsidies to council tenants as if these increased the burden on the taxpayer whilst tax concessions to owner-occupiers did not. The situation has become worse year after year as housing subsidies for rented houses are reduced whilst the cost of tax relief for house purchase increases at an ever more alarming rate. The cost was reported by ministers to be the gigantic sum of £7,700 million in 1990/91 for relief on mortgage interest alone. Since then the cost of relief has fallen, to £4,300 million in 1993/94, reflecting lower mortgage interest rates and the decision to limit relief to the basic rate of tax from April 1991. Hitherto higher rate tax payers had been entitled to mortgage interest relief at the higher rate despite the obvious fact that people who earn enough to be higher rate tax payers are in a better position to meet their housing costs without subsidy. The cost of relief was further reduced from April 1994 by the decision to cut to 20 per cent the rate at which relief is given, with the prospect of a further cut to 15 per cent in 1995.

The huge overall cost of interest relief was due to the rapid increase in the number of mortgaged home-owners in the 1980s, the very high interest rates in 1990/91 and the prevalence of endowment mortgages (which maximise entitlement to assistance). But it must be remembered that for individual home-owners there were factors at work which diminished the value of relief. First, relief is only available on the first £30,000 of any mortgage and this ceiling has not been increased since 1983. At that time the average new mortgage was £18,350 and by 1994 the average was £48,600. Second, falling income tax rates meant that tax relief also fell – in 1979 the basic rate of tax was 33 per cent compared with 25 per cent in the mid 1990s; for the rich the top rate of tax has been cut from 83 per cent in 1979 to 40 per cent now.

MIRAS

Before 1983, mortgagors got tax relief on mortgage interest by a reduction in their tax bill up to a permitted maximum. Someone liable only for tax at the standard rate got relief at the standard rate. Someone who paid tax at a higher rate got relief at the top rate.

In April 1983 the system was changed by the introduction of MIRAS (Mortgage interest relief at source). Mortgagors paid interest reduced by tax at the standard rate and the building societies were reimbursed by the Exchequer for lost income.

Other tax privileges for owner-occupiers

The sale of any asset normally results in liability to capital gains tax on any profits from the sale. Home-ownership, where the home is the principal dwelling of the seller, is exempt. The cost of this exemption was estimated by the Treasury to be worth £2,200 million in 1985-86. By 1988-89, after three years of steep increases in house prices, the estimate was £10,000 million, dwarfing even the huge cost of tax relief on mortgage interest, and making the cost of subsidies on council houses a mere bagatelle.

Owning a home as an investment

Ownership has conventionally been seen as a very good hedge against inflation, in that the house buyer's costs are mainly mortgage repayments and these are fixed, not on the current value of the dwelling but on the amount borrowed when the house was bought. It is this characteristic of home-ownership – annual costs based on the historic cost – that is its most important and valuable feature but only when prices are rising.

Consider someone who bought the average new house in 1975, the price being £12,000, interest then 11 per cent, loan period 25 years. That house today will fetch £50,000. Mortgage repayments will have fluctuated as interest rates have varied from 8.5 per cent to 15 per cent. Nevertheless, it has been putting on an average of £2,700 per year in value, over twice as much as the annual mortgage repayments ever since it was bought. And in a few years the mortgage repayments will end, leaving the owner with a debt-free, rent-free, high-value asset.

No wonder home-ownership has been highly regarded, and continues to be, despite the ravages of the slump in house prices in the early 1990s.

Other considerations

Since the house price bubble burst in 1988, we have seen another side to home-ownership. Some very painful lessons have been learned by people who have discovered by bitter personal experience that home-ownership is not a guaranteed route to wealth accumulation. A new term – negative equity – entered the language as people who had bought houses with high percentage mortgages at the peak of the prices spiral found that falling prices left them with debts which exceeded the value of their homes. The Bank of England estimated that 1 million home-owners were affected by negative equity in 1992 although others have put the figure at nearer 1.5 million.

Negative equity becomes a problem for borrowers when they want to sell their houses. As the recession of the early 1990s threw large numbers of people out of work, increasing numbers of borrowers found that they could neither afford to meet their mortgage repayments nor sell at a price that would cover the outstanding debt. The dream of home-ownership had turned into a nightmare for these unfortunate people who were simultaneously victims of both housing policy and economic recession.

Mortgage arrears of more than six months rose during the 1980s but really accelerated in the early 1990s. By 1992 over 350,000 borrowers were more than six months behind with their mortgage payments. Not surprisingly the lenders, which are, after all, commercial financial institutions, began to increase the rate at which they took houses into possession. In 1989 15,810 houses were taken into possession but the following year the figure jumped to 45,890 and then rose to an all time record of 75,540 in 1991. Since then things have improved somewhat and the latest figures indicate that levels of mortgage arrears are coming down as the economy recovers. However, the severity of the housing market slump following the absurdities of the boom must surely have dented people's faith in home-ownership. This may actually be a good thing if it helps to lower expectations and prevent the sort of speculative activity that led to the problems.

7 Reform: A Range of Views

I t is clear that reform of housing finance is urgently required. There are gross inequities between the different tenures and within them. The financial arrangements are inefficient and wasteful and, as such, impose a considerable burden on public funds.

Housing finance systems should be designed to meet a number of basic objectives against which they can be evaluated. The conventional objectives of housing policy, covering quantity, quality and price suggest that financial

arrangements should be put in place to produce an adequate supply of housing at prices (whether to rent or buy) that enable everyone to have access to a socially acceptable standard of accommodation. In addition, it is important that subsidies are equitably distributed, targeting help on those in need. There is also a strong case for saying that the financial framework should not lead people to choose one tenure rather than another.

In Britain, at the present time, there is a considerable shortfall in the supply of new housing for rent. Most independent estimates suggest that there is a need to provide 100,000 new rental dwellings each year but output by local authorities has been cut back to virtually nothing and the government's own target for housing association production meets only half the required total. In the private rented sector there have been claims of a revival of investment in new supply but the Business Expansion Scheme produced only 40,000 dwellings in five years and has been discontinued.

Turning to the quality of the stock, the latest estimates suggest that one dwelling in thirteen is unfit for human habitation, and that 'For owner occupied, privately rented and housing association homes the outstanding costs of meeting the comprehensive repair standard expected by building societies for mortgage purposes is at least £46 billion' (P Leather, S Mackintosh & S Rolfe, *Papering Over the Cracks*, 1994).

Affordability has been much debated in recent times although the government has steadfastly refused to say clearly what constitutes an affordable level of household expenditure on housing. The evidence shows that rents in all sectors have risen much faster than inflation in the last five years leading to serious questions being asked about whether the upward trend has now taken rents beyond an affordable level. The NFHA monitors rents of new lettings in the housing association sector and its figures for the fourth quarter of 1993 show that two thirds of cases failed the Federation's affordability test (see chapter 3).

Targeting of subsidy has improved in recent years as income related assistance has come to replace general (bricks and mortar) subsidy. However, there are now serious problems arising from the deep poverty trap generated by the way that benefit is withdrawn as income rises. Higher rent levels mean that people living on benefits suffer from powerful disincentives to find work.

The government has removed the grosser inequities that used to exist in the mortgage interest relief system whereby higher rate tax payers received a higher level of assistance with mortgage costs.

In 1974 the then Secretary of State for the Environment, Anthony Crosland, described British housing finance arrangements as a 'dog's breakfast' and it looked for a while as if there was sufficient political commitment to reform for something coherent and comprehensive to be put in place. However, the political situation soon changed and all that was achieved under the Labour government was the development of a new approach to council house subsidies.

During the 1980s there was a lot of debate about what could be done to reform housing finance. Academics working in the field generally constructed their proposals around the idea of 'tenure neutrality' which means that taxes and subsidies should be designed so that they do not have undue influence on people's housing choices. Attempts to design a tenure neutral housing finance system can take different forms but what they usually have in common is a commitment to reform across the board, affecting all tenures to a greater or lesser extent. In public debate, however, much attention focused on the issue of mortgage interest tax relief. Those who favoured reform concentrated on tax relief for two main reasons – the huge sums of money involved and the injustice of an aspect of housing finance that gave most help to the better off and least to the least well off.

Reform of tax relief was essential to any attempt to produce a housing finance system that gave adequate levels of assistance to those in greatest need without increasing the overall level of public expenditure. In 1985 support for reform came from a leading figure in the building society movement,

Tim Melville-Ross, who referred to 'our crazy system of housing finance subsidy which favours owner occupation to the detriment of every other form of tenure', and said that the way to a thorough and radical re-think of our housing policy is paved with the abolition of mortgage tax relief. The government of the day, however, remained stubbornly committed to the retention of tax relief, demonstrating how party political calculations can override technical and moral arguments.

The Duke of Edinburgh's report

In July 1985 there was a major contribution to the debate from a committee set up by the National Federation of Housing Associations and chaired by the Duke of Edinburgh. The *Inquiry into British Housing* attracted wide attention, much of it directed to one recommendation, that mortgage interest relief was not justified and should be phased out. This was a pity for it was only one of several equally important proposals. The value of the report was in its comprehensive survey of the situation, the arrangements which had produced it and the challenging solutions that were proposed. It recommended a form of tenure neutral housing finance system based on the phasing out of mortgage interest tax relief and the introduction of a needs related housing allowance and capital value rents in all rented sectors.

The needs related allowance would replace the tangle of subsidies, housing benefit and mortgage interest tax relief. It would extend to low income owner-occupiers who continue to be a neglected group. The fact that the creation of the allowance entailed the phasing out of tax relief ensured that in the political climate of the mid-1980s the package was instantly rejected by the government – the then prime minister, Margaret Thatcher, remained committed to the retention of tax relief right up until her departure from office in 1990.

The Inquiry's recommendation for rents was that tenants in all sectors should pay rents based on four per cent of the current capital value of their home (assuming vacant possession) plus an allowance for management and maintenance. This would give comparability across all rented dwellings and while rents would be set to give a reasonable return they would not be as high as in an unregulated market. It was claimed that rents set on this basis would be sufficient to attract new capital investment into private renting.

Capital value rents would result in big increases for many tenants and it was accepted that the introduction of the needs related allowance was a necessary precondition of the new approach. Indeed the recommendations of the Inquiry team were clearly set out as a package:

'Our central recommendations hang together as a unity: they are not a checklist from which some parts, but not others, can be extracted.'

The report criticised successive governments for making piecemeal decisions and failing to face up to the challenge of coherent, across the board reform. And it was precisely because the Inquiry report put forward a package that it was rejected by a government that preferred to pursue its radical objectives by revealing only one step at a time.

The Duke's second report

In 1990 the Inquiry team reconvened and after further deliberation published a second report in June 1991. The second report essentially relaunched the package of proposals contained in the 1985 report but it also went on to argue for a series of further measures designed to reverse the continuing decline in the overall availability of rented housing. In the local authority sector, the report called for recognition that the ring-fencing of the housing revenue account had changed the relationship between housing and other local services. It was argued that the logic of treating the landlord function as separate from other local authority accounts meant that government should go one step further and treat local authority landlords in a similar way to independent housing associations. This would give local housing authorities freedom to raise private finance, secured against the value of the stock.

However, the report recognised the difficulties of challenging the rigid Treasury conventions on public expenditure and went on to suggest that it might be necessary to introduce 'transfers of engagements' in order to get round the restrictions. This would mean transferring the ownership of all the assets and liabilities of the housing stock to financially independent bodies. The idea of 'local housing companies' was followed up in a report commissioned by the Joseph Rowntree Foundation and is discussed later in this chapter.

The Duke's second report also suggested an end to the system, introduced in the Local Government and Housing Act 1989, whereby most local authorities receive housing benefit payments for their tenants reduced by notional HRA surpluses. This was a welcome recognition of the fact that housing benefit is a social security payment, not a housing subsidy. Private landlords and housing associations receive rental income based on full payment of housing benefit and only local authorities are penalised in this way.

Taken together the two reports of the *Inquiry into British Housing* represent a major contribution to the debate about the reform of housing finance. However, their impact on government policy has been negligible – timing and political influence, it seems, are almost more important than a convincing set of arguments.

Faith in the City

Published in December 1985, *Faith in the City* was a report of the Archbishop of Canterbury's Commission on Urban Priority Areas. The report took a different approach from that of the *Inquiry into British Housing*. It addressed itself to the social considerations on which housing policy should be based, to the principles which should inform the attitudes and actions of government and ourselves. The importance of the report lay in its examination of the fundamental deficiencies of existing policies and thinking which had brought us to the present situation.

Our society, the report said, had accepted that every citizen has a right to at least a basic standard of living guaranteed through social security, free education and health care. Housing, however, is as fundamental to human development as health care yet it has never been accepted as a right for all. Although public housing was originally intended, with much success, to break the connection between low income and poor housing, it has never been adequately funded. Supply has never met demand and, too often, council housing has been regarded as 'housing suitable for poor people'. And in the last 15 years, that link between poverty and poor housing has been re-established and strengthened.

As for the private rented sector, it flourished when costs and interest rates were low but investment in further provision dried up long ago. *Faith in the City* saw no future for an expansion of this tenure.

The voluntary housing movement had made only a small contribution to the national housing stock, the Commission found, but had an excellent record in its initiatives and in catering for special needs. It could be a significant force for the future but its financial dependence made it increasingly subject to government policy.

Faith in the City noted that the government relied heavily on home-ownership, claiming that it was the best way to promote consumer choice. However, the Commission felt that what characterised the housing conditions of the poor was lack of choice; and while owner-occupation did give maximum choice to those who could afford it, and made good financial sense for them, it could never be available and appropriate to everyone.

In pointing the way forward, the Commission concluded that the housing problem cannot be contained, let alone reversed, without an expanded rented housing programme. In practice, housing was being made to bear the brunt of public expenditure cuts with no sign at that time of any revival of investment in private renting.

Better standards were needed. A home is more than bricks and mortar, a roof over one's head. Decent housing means a place that is dry, warm and in a reasonable state of repair. It also means security, privacy, sufficient space, a place where people can grow, make choices, become whole people. The standards for public housing were ungenerous in space and appeared to assume that all the household except the woman and young children were out all day.

Faith in the City reminded us not merely of the size of the physical challenge, and the inequity and inefficiency of present arrangements, but also of the critical importance of decent housing to a just society; in short, the thinking that should shape the reforms which are so urgently needed. These things inevitably cost money, but the Commission pointed out that if housing was regarded as a priority, money would become available.

Housing and the economy

One of the most important developments in the debate about housing and the reform of housing finance in Britain in recent years has been the growing recognition of the significance of the links between housing and the wider economy. This is an area where Shelter has played an influential part in taking the analysis of academic economists to a wider audience. The wild fluctuations in the economy, and even more marked ups and downs in the housing market in the 1980s, undoubtedly stimulated much of this work. After 1979 the government stoked up demand for home-ownership so that by the end of the 1980s two thirds of the population were in this tenure. At the same time the government set about deregulating financial services, making it much easier to obtain credit. The deregulation of banking in the early '80s led to the ending of the building societies' interest rate cartel, ending mortgage queues, and leading to the Building Societies Act, 1986. Together with rising real incomes as the economy recovered from the recession of 1981 there was strong upward pressure on house prices and as people saw the value of their assets increase so they were encouraged to turn their wealth into increased demand for consumer goods.

The combination of larger numbers of home-owners and much increased house values created a vast amount of unused equity and dramatically increased the importance of the housing market in the economy as a whole. Economists such as John Muellbauer (ROOF, May + June 1990) provided powerful explanations of what was happening. Muellbauer argued that by letting house prices rise so fast in 1986-88 the government committed one of the biggest blunders of economic management in the whole of the post-war period.

Muellbauer added his voice to those calling for the reform of mortgage tax relief, suggesting what he called a self-financing system. Entitlement to relief would be limited to the first eight to ten years of a loan, and the cost of this would be covered by a tax levied on home-owners with more mature loans. He also suggested that home loans should be given a higher risk rating – subsequent experience has shown this to be entirely justified – and that lenders should provide lower proportions of purchase prices. This would require purchasers to save bigger deposits and help to prevent the kind of mad rush to borrow that occurs when housing markets are booming.

The importance of the work by Muellbauer and others is that it draws attention to the need for policy makers to recognise that the housing market has great influence on the course of the economy and vice versa. And this does a lot to raise the prominence of housing in public debate.

Local housing companies

One of the major developments in housing policy in the late 1980s was the government's rediscovery of the need for rented housing. After nearly a decade of emphasising home-ownership as the answer to all housing problems, the Conservative Party at last recognised that there were limits to the number of people for whom owner-occupation was appropriate. This led to the increase in funds for housing association development, and to direct support for new investment in private rented housing. Local authorities, however, continued to be frozen out of government thinking despite the fact that they were the owners of four million dwellings – a hugely valuable asset base which could provide the basis of an investment programme yielding exceptionally good value for money.

It was local authorities themselves who developed the idea of large scale voluntary transfer (LSVT) whereby all the stock of council houses in an area is transferred to a new owner — so far nearly always housing associations set up specially for this purpose. By mid-1994 around 32 English local authorities had transferred all their stock in this way. LSVT is an approach that requires the new owner to raise sufficient private capital to buy the stock and even as the LSVT model was being developed other ideas were being discussed, avoiding the need to raise large amounts of loan finance.

The most detailed work on local housing companies has been carried out by Steve Wilcox and others for the Joseph Rowntree Foundation (*Local Housing Companies: New Opportunities for Council Housing*, 1993). The key objectives for local housing companies set out in this report are:

- to facilitate an increase in social housing investment without increasing net public expenditure;
- to provide local housing authorities, both large and small, with a means of competing on equal terms with housing associations;
- to maintain local accountability both to the local authority and to tenants.

These objectives can be pursued by means of companies set up by local authorities to own and manage the housing stock. The report reminds us that in the past British local authorities set up arm's length companies to run trading services and in some cases to carry out housing redevelopment activities. The key idea in the modern version is that council housing could be transferred to a new landlord body as a going concern without the need to raise very large amounts of capital to purchase the properties. The new company would simply take on the financial responsibility for the outstanding debt on the stock; the great advantage would be that it would be free to raise as much private finance as was needed to maintain, improve and add to the stock without that borrowing counting as public expenditure. The local council could retain an involvement in the management of the new company and places on the board could be available for tenants as well as independent members recruited for their financial or other relevant skills.

The local housing companies idea has found support from across a wide political spectrum, from Labour's Social Justice Commission to the Director of the CBI, and at the time of writing (June 1994) seems to point towards a positive future for public housing.

Housing and social justice

During the 1980s right wing think tanks such as the Adam Smith Institute exercised tremendous influence on the government, giving us, amongst other things, the poll tax. It was partly to counter the influence of these tiny but powerful organisations that the Institute for Public Policy Research (IPPR)was set up in 1988 by a group of left-leaning figures in the academic, business and trade union communities. In 1994 it published *Housing and Social Justice* (edited by R Goodlad and K Gibb) which contains a number of specific proposals for the reform of housing finance. There is much in common between these proposals and those of the two reports of the *Inquiry into British Housing*, including, as already mentioned, support for the idea of local housing companies.

The authors call for the reform of housing finance designed to make the system more equitable and efficient and align themselves with the many voices calling for a proper reform of mortgage interest tax relief – as distinct from merely phasing it out. What is required, they argue, is the redeployment of the resources saved from tax relief to introduce a mortgage benefit scheme, with the longer term objective of a more comprehensive housing allowance scheme.

They also line up with those who recognise a need for a properly functioning private rented sector – to facilitate mobility and to support a move to lower percentage loans for first-time buyers. In order to support even a small, healthy private rented sector, they say, the government needs to introduce depreciation allowances, license approved landlords (to reassure tenants) and provide a durable subsidy to assist private landlords earn adequate rates of return.

On the question of sources of investment finance to support the development of social rented housing, they support the idea launched by an earlier IPPR report for a new housing bank to be set up. This would channel capital receipts from council house sales and act as a capitalised financial intermediary to inject private finance into associations and local housing companies.

Housing benefit is recognised as a major area for reform. The current housing benefit system is deeply flawed in a number of ways, the main one being the depth of the poverty trap created by the policy of moving ever closer to complete reliance on personal income related forms of support instead of traditional bricks and mortar subsidies. The authors of the IPPR report call for short-term reforms designed to combine their new mortgage benefit with a dual taper housing benefit but they see this as only temporary, pending more fundamental reform of the benefits system.

This chapter has looked at a range of views expressed over the last ten years or so about how Britain's chaotic and unfair housing finance system could be reformed. It is clear that there are some areas of substantial agreement, at least in broad terms. What has been lacking has been the political will to embrace a coherent, equitable and durable package of reforms.

8 What Next?

Much change, little reform

The government has not adopted the kind of reform referred to in the previous chapter and has been openly scornful of some of the ideas put forward. But that does not mean it has neglected the issue; on the contrary, over the 15 years since the Conservatives took office, they have been very actively involved in legislating on a number of aspects of housing finance. There have been:

- two new subsidy systems for council housing,
- two attempts to recast the rent rebate (housing benefit) system,
- new controls on local authority capital expenditure,
- a new financial regime for housing associations,
- deregulation of private renting,
- an experiment with tax breaks for investors in private renting,
- major changes to the financial environment within which building societies operate and, at last,
- a real breakthrough on the issue of mortgage interest relief.

What needs to be appreciated here is that all these changes do not add up to a coherent reform of housing finance based on a commitment to greater equity and efficiency. But neither are they completely incoherent – the government does know what it is doing. Its housing finance policies have been driven by three main factors. First, the Conservative government has been deeply committed to the rapid growth of home-ownership, partly because of the Party's belief in the virtues of private market solutions to all problems and partly because of a crude party political calculation that more home-owners meant more Tory voters. As a result of this commitment, the reform of housing finance has been anti-council housing and tilted very much in favour of reinforcing demand for home-ownership rather than constructing a system that was equitable, economically efficient and tenure neutral. This is why the reform of tax relief was so staunchly resisted by Margaret Thatcher for so long.

Second, there has been a consistent preference for personal, income related subsidies over bricks and mortar subsidies, in both the council and housing association sectors. And this is itself related to the wish to move rents in all sectors towards market levels in order to help revive private renting.

Third, housing policies over the last 15 years have been heavily influenced by the Treasury and its attempts to control or reduce public expenditure. The importance of the Treasury cannot be overstated in the context of housing policy and other programme areas. Thus, whilst the government has at last moved to reduce tax relief in recent budgets, it has done so with the intention of reducing the overall budget deficit and not in the context of a plan to redistribute resources into a fairer mortgage benefit system.

From the vantage point of the mid-1990s, we can see that although 15 years of Tory rule has produced considerable change in housing finance it has produced at least as many problems as it has solved. In many ways the housing crisis is worse now than it was in the late 1970s. The insistence on the sale of council houses has led to a huge reduction in the supply of rented accommodation and the forced ending of new building by local authorities has only made this worse.

Policies designed to shift the subsidy burden from bricks and mortar to personal assistance have created a savage poverty trap for millions of low income households. A government which has reduced to 40 per cent the top level of tax for the rich has raised to 97 per cent the 'tax' rate applied to some people moving from benefit into work. The Party of incentives and individual responsibility has eliminated all work incentives for the poorest and reinforced the very dependency that it sought to remove.

Pushing housing associations into the grip of private financial institutions has forced rents to rise and has threatened the long-term viability of associations as effective developers of new affordable rented housing. Despite all the efforts of the government over 15 years, it was only the collapse of the owner-occupier market after 1988 that eventually led to a measurable increase in the supply of accommodation in this sector – and much of this increase is expected to melt away again if and when the market recovers.

It is a sad indictment of the Tories' record over four parliaments that the Party more committed to home-ownership than any other in British history is also the Party that has presided over the deepest and longest housing market recession in living memory. The record levels of mortgage arrears and houses taken into possession, together with the emergence of widespread negative equity problems bear grim testimony to the misguided nature of government policy on housing and the wider economy. The statistics record the numbers of victims of government policies which have pumped up home-ownership way beyond prudent limits.

Housing policy under the Conservatives has been undermined by the obsession with home-ownership as the solution to virtually all problems, the blind faith in the power of market forces and the belief that private enterprise is always superior to public services. The unending and unjustified assault on local government and the retention of irrational public spending conventions have only made matters worse.

What ought to be happening

There has to be a change of thinking and attitudes of whatever government is in power, if the present crisis is to end. The unlikelihood of a change of course by the present government is no reason for avoiding a consideration of what these changes might be. For many years the main obstacle to coherent reform of housing finance has been political rather than technical. But the Tories have had long enough to put their policies into effect, long enough for their failure to be clear to everyone. In a very real sense the failure of policy is one of the strongest cards in the hand of those who advocate reform.

There is a number of points to be made in outlining the shape of reform now needed. In the broadest terms, what is required is a level of competence in economic management that will avoid the disastrous cycle of boom and slump which has been so damaging to the housing market in recent years. Economic stability could lead to greater stability in house prices and it would surely be a good thing if people were encouraged to think less about how much wealth they could accumulate through home-ownership.

Measures more specifically related to housing and housing finance need to stimulate supply (for both renting and owner-occupation) and investment in repair and improvement. They also need to distribute subsidy in ways that are seen to be fairer and more efficient than at present while ensuring that rents are affordable and without intense poverty trap problems.

It is clear that the present framework for the supply of new rented housing is not sustainable in the long term. Some housing associations may be in a position in the short term to build at lower grant rates but it will not be long before debt will reach a level that puts further investment in jeopardy. Some solution has be found. A return to higher levels of housing association grant would be one sensible way forward, and this would fit in with demands for greater emphasis on bricks and mortar subsidies as a way to tackle the poverty trap and affordability issues.

Another way to revive investment in new rented housing would be to release the capital receipts mountain owned by local authorities as a result of right to buy sales. This is something that has been regularly demanded over a number of years and there is no justification for the government denying councils the right to use their own receipts. However, accumulated capital receipts would not meet the need in the longer term and something else is required.

Local authorities have a pivotal role to play in the future of social rented housing as any less ideologically blinkered government would have perceived years ago. Local authority housing represents a huge asset which could be used to raise the finance for future investment; the problem is how to unlock the potential and to get round Treasury rules on public expenditure and restrictions on local authority involvement. The idea of local housing companies has been mentioned in the previous chapter and now seems to be generating a wide base of support from across the political spectrum. The attraction of the local housing company idea is that it could give access to the necessary investment funds without having to raise large amounts of money to buy the stock in the first place. It is an idea which also permits the retention of a significant degree of local authority participation and local accountability.

Turning to questions of pricing and subsidy, the problem here is that the government has created a situation in which people have been encouraged to see home-ownership as the natural tenure for the majority and renting is seen as either a short-term option for people on their way to buying a house or a long-term provision for people who cannot afford to buy. Thus rented housing, especially local authority and housing association stock, caters for a lot of people on very low incomes. In this situation there really is very little point in the policy of ever higher rents.

The government has deliberately pursued a policy of forcing rents to rise, shifting the burden of subsidy from bricks and mortar to housing benefit. It can hardly complain, therefore, when the housing benefit bill rises steeply. One of the main reasons for the move towards market rents for all sectors was that it would help to stimulate the supply of private renting. This is a case of allowing the tail to wag the dog and it has clearly failed. Deregulation of rents was a piece of Tory ideology which should be reversed by a future government as a matter of urgency.

What is also required here is a commitment to a cross-tenure reform which would embrace both housing benefit and mortgage interest relief. Such a reform would utilise the resources released from mortgage interest relief to fund a more equitable benefit available to low income household in all tenures.

The difficulties of achieving the necessary reforms in British housing finance should not be underestimated. But neither should the difficulties become an excuse for inaction. There is much to be done but, as this book has shown, a lot of changes have been made over the last 15 years, proving that the system can be reformed if the political will is there.

Index